You may not agree with Jessie Minassian on every point, but I love her courage and compassion. If you need straight talk delivered with a loving voice, absolutely read *Unashamed*.

**NANCY RUE**
Author of *The Merciful Scar* and *The Whole Guy Thing*

Like a cold glass of water in a squelching desert, Jessie Minassian is a refreshing voice in a voiceless land. Authentic. Clear. Engaging. Biblical. Jessie cuts to the heart of what teenage girls need to hear in these turbulent times. If you're a teenage girl, or are trying to parent one, you absolutely cannot afford to pass up this book!

**PRESTON SPRINKLE, PHD**
Vice President of Eternity Bible College's Boise extension and author of *Fight*, *Erasing Hell*, and *Charis*

This is a vital book for parents and teen girls alike. Jessie Minassian's vulnerable, authentic call to live in freedom from the sins that so easily entangle will be a powerful encouragement to girls who think they can never break free from these "secret sins," and an empowering discussion-starter for parents wondering what in the world their daughters are going through. Read this book!

**MARK GREGSTON**
Founder and executive director of Heartlight Ministries

Working with teenage girls on a weekly basis and having dealt with some of the same issues Jessie Minassian discusses, I very much appreciate her honesty and detail as she hits big topics such as cutting, eating disorders, etc., bringing sin and shame into the light. Isolation in our struggles can be crippling, but she lets us know we are not alone. Teenage girls should read this, as should parents and mentors—and the discussion questions are a great asset. We have probably all been there or known someone close to us in these situations. Now as parents and mentors we have more support through *Unashamed: Overcoming the Sins No Girl Wants to Talk About* to better understand these topics, pass on wisdom, and hopefully help our girls bypass some of the sin and shame that holds so many in bondage.

**LAURA HAIRSTON**
Executive director of Forge America

While you may not agree with everything written, this book is still very good. Jessie's encouragement to the reader to go to a parent, family member, or someone older to hold them accountable is very wise counsel. This book may serve as a great tool for many young women and moms to see the ugliness of "sins." Moms in particular, don't be too busy or ashamed of your daughter to help her deal with these issues. The world is seducing our girls. It is heart wrenching to think that there is such a great need for a book like this.

**IRENE GARCIA**
Author of *Rich in Love*, mother of eighteen

# OVERCOMING THE SINS NO GIRL WANTS TO TALK ABOUT

Jessie Minassian

UNashamed

Beatrice—
Live Unashamed!
♥ Jessie

NAVPRESS

A NavPress resource published in alliance
with Tyndale House Publishers, Inc.

# NAVPRESS⊘®

NavPress is the publishing ministry of The Navigators, an international Christian organization and leader in personal spiritual development. NavPress is committed to helping people grow spiritually and enjoy lives of meaning and hope through personal and group resources that are biblically rooted, culturally relevant, and highly practical.

**For more information, visit www.NavPress.com.**

*Unashamed: Overcoming the Sins No Girl Wants to Talk About*

Copyright © 2015 by Jessie Minassian. All rights reserved.

A NavPress resource published in alliance with Tyndale House Publishers, Inc.

*NAVPRESS* and the NAVPRESS logo are registered trademarks of NavPress, The Navigators, Colorado Springs, CO. *TYNDALE* is a registered trademark of Tyndale House Publishers, Inc. Absence of ® in connection with marks of NavPress or other parties does not indicate an absence of registration of those marks.

Cover design by Nicole Grimes

Cover photograph taken by Stephen Vosloo. Copyright © by Tyndale House Publishers, Inc. All rights reserved.

Author photo taken by Open Sky Photography, copyright © 2014. All rights reserved.

Published in association with the literary agency of Wolgemuth & Associates, Inc.

Names have been changed throughout to protect the privacy of the individuals. If actual names were used, permission was received. All stories are used with permission.

Unless otherwise indicated, all Scripture quotations are taken from the *Holy Bible*, New Living Translation, copyright © 1996, 2004, 2007, 2013 by Tyndale House Foundation. Used by permission of Tyndale House Publishers, Inc., Carol Stream, Illinois 60188. All rights reserved.

Scripture quotations marked MSG are taken from *THE MESSAGE* by Eugene H. Peterson, copyright © 1993, 1994, 1995, 1996, 2000, 2001, 2002. Used by permission of NavPress Publishing Group. All rights reserved.

Scripture quotations marked HCSB are taken from the Holman Christian Standard Bible,® copyright © 1999, 2000, 2002, 2003, 2009 by Holman Bible Publishers. Used by permission. Holman Christian Standard Bible,® Holman CSB,® and HCSB® are federally registered trademarks of Holman Bible Publishers.

Scripture quotations marked NIV are taken from the Holy Bible, *New International Version,*® *NIV.*® Copyright © 1973, 1978, 1984, 2011 by Biblica, Inc.® Used by permission. All rights reserved worldwide.

Library of Congress Cataloging-in-Publication Data

Minassian, Jessie.
    Unashamed : overcoming the sins no girl wants to talk about / Jessie Minassian.
        pages cm
    Includes bibliographical references.
    ISBN 978-1-61291-628-6
1. Guilt—Religious aspects—Christianity.    2. Forgiveness of sin.    3. Women—Religious life.    I. Title.
    BT722.M56 2015
    248.8'33—dc23                                                                                           2014034224

Printed in the United States of America

| 21 | 20 | 19 | 18 | 17 | 16 | 15 |
|----|----|----|----|----|----|----|
| 7  | 6  | 5  | 4  | 3  | 2  | 1  |

THOSE WHO LOOK TO HIM FOR HELP WILL BE *radiant* *with* *joy*; NO SHADOW OF SHAME WILL DARKEN THEIR FACES. Psalm 34:5

To the God who drove away my
shame with His radiant light.

And to E. H.—your story isn't finished.

# Contents

# A Note to Parents

Parenting daughters in the twenty-first century may be one of the greatest challenges ever faced by humankind. I know; I'm a parent of girls too. As guardians of our daughters' purity, you and I have to navigate a maze of media, friends, and other potentially harmful influences and teach our girls how to think, act, and love God on their own.

I wrote *Unashamed* because I care about your daughters and mine. I wrote it because sometimes, despite our best efforts, our daughters get trapped by sin they don't know how to ditch. Girls are really good at hiding their brokenness—so good, in fact, that most feel they are all alone in their struggles. The sheer number of girls trapped by "secret sins"—eating disorders, cutting, sexual addiction, substance abuse, same-sex relationships—might surprise you. In fact, it might blow you away. Statistically, there's a very good chance that either your daughter or someone she knows is caught up in something on that list.

If you're wondering whether *Unashamed* is an appropriate

read for your daughter, I applaud you for being careful. I've chosen to talk about sin in a frank and conversational way in this book because I know from personal experience that secrecy fuels shame and perpetuates addiction. If your daughter is exposed to secular media (TV, movies, music, magazines), I doubt anything in this book will shock or surprise her. However, as her parent, only you can decide whether the contents of *Unashamed* would be helpful. I care deeply for your daughter, and my goal is to see her (and equip her to help others to) live in freedom.

# Introduction

I've read a lot of books—*lots* of them—and all my favorites have something in common. Each one made me feel as if I were talking with a friend or at least someone who cared about my life. I guess when it comes down to it, I don't like having someone I've never met tell me how to live. Wild guess here: maybe you don't either? It's easier to listen to advice when we hear it from someone we know and who we know cares about us, right? (And let's be honest, sometimes it's really encouraging to hear that an author is *human*, just like the rest of us!) So before we dig into this book together, it's only fair that we get to know each other a bit.

I'm Jessie. My given name is actually Jessica, and my last name is so hard to pronounce that I avoid using it when possible. (Just for kicks, it's pronounced min-à-see-in.) My single momma brought me into this world on a beautiful Californian March day just a *few* years ago (wink). She got married when I was five, and I grew up in a blended family of five kids. I played lots of sports in school and tried to figure out how to love God with my whole heart when it seemed to be *way* more interested in boys. I liked school when I had friends, thought it was miserable when I didn't. I got good grades, ate too many Twix for lunch, and never got used to spending ten to twelve hours a week on a school bus. (We lived kind of in the boondocks.)

After high school graduation, I went to a Christian college in Southern California. I played volleyball there and then got into rock climbing. I studied abroad two semesters, one in Israel and the other in Costa Rica. I still liked school when I had friends and learned not to be miserable when I didn't. I got fewer good grades, stopped eating Twix for lunch, and traded the school bus for my first car (a ridiculously small, gold Toyota MR2). There were ups, there were downs, and then there was *him*.

I married my match made in heaven the weekend after college graduation. For now, let me just say that Paul (or "Paco," as most people know him) swept me off my feet and I have never looked back. Best friends make the best soul mates, and he was—and is—both. (*Awww!*) I didn't think I had room for any more love in my heart until God gave us two daughters, Ryan and Logan. They're sweet li'l blessings wrapped in two feisty packages!

Besides loving on my family, my greatest joy these days is to help girls find their identity, pleasure, and purpose in God. I'm the resident big sis for a website called LifeLoveandGod.com, where I answer girls' questions about . . . well, life, love, and God. (I know, pretty creative, right?) Now that I have two daughters of my own, I'm all the more passionate about seeing girls understand their unique beauty, know how amazing God is, and hold their heads high in dignity.

That's where the LIFE, LOVE & GOD books come in. These books are meant to be the closest thing to just hanging out at my house, going for a hike together, or meeting for a small group in my living room. Each book covers different stuff you're facing, whether it's relationships with guys, body image issues, or making sense of your family life.

You'll want to have a notebook or journal handy for the discussion questions at the end of each chapter. Trust me, you'll get so much more out of this book if you take time to think through those questions. Even better, grab a couple of friends (or your mom or a youth-group leader) and go through the book together! My heart is to see you grow in your relationship with God and shine with confidence, and that happens most often when you're in community with others.

You can find out more about my random favorite things on the "Meet Jessie" page at LifeLoveandGod.com. I'd love to hear a little about you, too, if you'd like to send me an e-mail through the website!

Whether you're caught in a cycle of sin yourself or just want to know how to help the silent sufferers all around you, let this be the beginning of your journey toward health and healing. God longs for you to live in the freedom He died for, and I want to be here for you in that journey!

Love,

*Jessie*

## CHAPTER 1

# The Silent Sufferers

*I was a silent sufferer.*

We might as well get this out of the way up front. Instead of leaving your curiosity spinning the entire book, wondering what juicy secret I'm hiding, I'm just going to air my dirty laundry on the first page. Sometimes it's best to tackle the hardest things first, right? Kind of like jumping into the deep end of the pool instead of inching in slowly, or pulling off a wax strip in one fell swoop instead of hair by hair. Why delay the pain? I'm just going to take a chance and lay it out there for you.

I was trapped by a sexual addiction for thirteen years.

It all started when I was seven. A friend showed me a

cartoonish "birds and bees" anatomy book her parents gave her and then pressured me to masturbate or she "wouldn't be my friend" anymore. (Great friend, right?) Not long after, a bully of an eight-year-old made me lie on top of her and do the same. I was so ashamed and so embarrassed that I never told anyone, not even my mom, who I trusted with everything. I *hated* what they had made me do, but I became addicted to the feeling. And it didn't take long for that addiction to cripple me inside. Their sin against me, wrong all on its own, introduced me to a sin that was wrong all on my own.[1] I hid the addiction well. By day I was an outgoing, God-loving girl, but by night I was a sin-crippled, shame-filled mess.

My heart was convicted that masturbation was wrong, so I fought against it.[2] Well, I tried to, ~~most~~ some of the time. But the truth is, I was way out of my league. I loved God, and I was a "good girl" in so many ways, but I was fighting a losing battle. Sexual addiction takes some serious ammo to slay, and I had no idea how to kill it. And my failure killed *me*. I tried—don't get me wrong. In fact, I went through seasons where I "did better." There were even times when I thought I was *all* better. But then I'd go back to my vice—like a dog to its own puke (see Proverbs 26:11)—and the fall would be twice as hard.

*Hypocrite. Sicko. Dirty girl.* The self-imposed labels stuck good and tight, glued to my heart with a nice big dose of shame.

The cycle went on for a long, long time: sin, repent,

try harder, sin, repent, try harder, over and over again. Life marched on: junior high, high school, college, boyfriends, missions trips, and dance recitals came and went. I played sports, won awards, started Bible studies—lived a completely normal life on the outside. I appeared to be just fine to everyone watching. But for all those years, inside I was caught in a sin cycle that spun so reliably that it would make a washing machine jealous. It affected my view of myself, but more important, it had a detrimental effect on my relationship with God.

But here's the good news—the *really, really* good news (and boy am I glad to finally get to this part!): I found freedom from my sin—real, genuine, not-going-back-to-that-mudhole-ever-again F-R-E-E-D-O-M. And can I just tell you that it's so good to be free? It's like nothing else on earth. Once you taste that kind of freedom, after years and years of crippling shame, it's like the feeling you get when you walk outside for the first time after being in bed puking your guts out for a few days. You walk feebly out the door, breathe in that crisp air, feel the sun on your cheeks, and then swear on your dead cat's grave that you'll never take another day of health for granted *ever* again. Freedom from a habitual, secret sin is like that—times ten.

So that's my story (at least the part of my life that applies to this book, and happily, there was—and *is*—much more to my life story than my secret sin!).

I was a silent sufferer, *and there's a good chance you're one too.* Maybe you try to numb your pain with a bottle, razor blade, or pill. Maybe you're addicted to pornography or shoplifting. Maybe your insecurities get all up in your head so you starve yourself or purge to be thin. Maybe you're attracted to other girls. Maybe you're in a sexual relationship with your boyfriend. Maybe your struggle is with more than one secret sin. I could spout off all sorts of statistics that prove you're likely to struggle with at least *something* on that list, but I don't think it would be especially helpful or needed. For one, you likely already know just how many girls struggle with one or more of these issues. Two, if you don't, a quick Google search should bring you up to speed. And three, the statistics are rising so fast, my current data would be obsolete by Tuesday. So instead of wasting space here on stats, I'd rather just get to the point: *You're not alone.*

If you're a silent sufferer, there's also a good chance you're not getting help because you're too scared of what people would think if they "knew." Maybe you think, like I did, that you're the only one on the planet who struggles with something so shameful, so you go on suffering in silence—*trapped* in silence. But as long as you suffer and sin in silence, you will never find the freedom that Christ died to offer you—the freedom I found and the freedom I want to help you discover.

There is part of me that really, *really* doesn't want to start this book with an indelible record of my secret sin. I realize that putting all this on paper for the world to read means that everyone—from complete strangers to my best friends—are going to know about my past. They might judge me. They might misunderstand me. They might think differently of me. And when I think about my two precious, innocent daughters reading this book someday? I'm not gonna lie: It makes me tear up just thinking about it. Someday my children will know that their momma struggled with *that*. Yeah, there's part of me that wants desperately to "select all" and "delete" right about now. But I'm not going to, and I'll tell you why.

From the world's perspective, I'd have to be crazy, drunk, or just plain stupid to volunteer information about my secret sins to the masses. But there's method to my madness, and it has everything to do with *you*. I care about you. The reason I chose to confess my sin at the very beginning of this book is so that you know you have nothing to hide. See, I've been helping girls overcome secret sins for a lot of years now, and the number one, biggest lie that Satan gets girls to believe is that they are rogue sinners—that they're out there sinning *on their own*. He wants you to think that you're the only one on the planet who struggles with something that gross or stupid or unforgivable. He wants you to cower alone in embarrassment. He wants you to hide out in fear. He wants you to wallow in shame. Why? Because he knows that if he can isolate you, his battle is half won. *That's* why I'm willing to risk vulnerability. I want to empower you with the truth that you are not alone!

We're going to look at a variety of secret sins in the next chapter, but before we get there, I want to talk about one common denominator between all of them. No matter what your struggle, one of Satan's favorite kinds of ammo—one of his biggest missiles—is shame. That's why I want to begin our journey toward freedom by talking about it.

## The Problem of Shame

I think I'm going to have to start out here by explaining exactly what I mean by the word *shame*. See, there's a type of shame we probably need a little bit more of in this world. There's a good kind of shame—a natural emotion that comes from doing something we know we shouldn't do. Here's an example.

In the fine city of San Francisco, they had to put an official citywide ban on nudity because of the excess number of "naturists" who would walk down the street sans pants, ride the bus in the buff, or chill in the city square getting some air down there. Seriously—that's just wrong. Who wants to sit on a bus seat that just had some old guy's sweaty cheeks rubbing all over it? Sick. Yet when the city voted (narrowly!) to ban public nudity except at certain festivals, a bunch of protestors angrily stripped down in the courthouse to let the whole world know how unfair the new "clothes on" rule was.[3] Now, can we just say it together? *People, have you no shame?!* Healthy shame is the kind that tells us it's a good thing to keep our booties and ta-tas covered up. (I'm well aware that before sin entered the world, Adam and Eve were plumb naked and felt no hint of shame—and good for them! But sin *has* entered the world, and now clothes should be a part of our daily routine.)

God put a mechanism in the human heart that lets us know when we're in the wrong. It's called a conscience, and that little human feature sounds the alarm when we stray from God and His way of living. Just so we're clear, He installed it on purpose (so it's a good thing to listen to it and not stifle it). Your conscience produces a whole spectrum of emotions—regret, embarrassment, fear, and yes, *shame*—when we violate God's Law. By definition, shame is "a painful emotion caused by consciousness of guilt, shortcoming, or impropriety."[4] In other words, when we know we've done wrong, we feel it down deep.[5] That can be a good thing! In chapter 6, we're going to see how feeling sorry about our sin can be beneficial and how you can use those emotions to your advantage. But for now, we just need to understand that there *is* a normal kind of shame that is (or should be) par for the course when we do stupid stuff (see Ezekiel 36:31-32).

That said, when we talk about shame in the context of this book, I'll be referring to a different kind of shame. It's a debilitating, overboard type of emotion that cripples and haunts you. It's the kind of shame that tells you you're beyond redemption—that you're too far gone and far too gross for even God to love. *That* kind of shame isolates, crushes, and leaves you for dead. That kind of shame allows Satan to win.

McKenna[6] is one of the beautiful "little sisters" I've been blessed to counsel, pray for, and cry with. McKenna is a silent sufferer, allegorically and, for a time, quite literally. The sexual abuse she endured at the hand of an older coworker left her unable to speak for a long time. She came to LifeLoveandGod.com consumed with shame over the abuse and also the fact that it led to a sexual addiction she still struggles with today. Sin and shame have a way of tearing us up and stealing our joy, and by the time I met McKenna, she was in a dark place. I recently asked her to think back to that time in her life. She shared,

> After the abuse, I continued to [sin] because I believed that I was permanently dirty and sinful anyway. The sin caused me to push away from God for a while because I felt too sinful and ashamed. Even now, sometimes I feel like I'm irredeemable and figure that I can never heal from my sin even if I stop.

I appreciate her honesty so much! And it goes without saying that she's not the only one who feels that way.

Note: I'm happy to say that McKenna's story isn't finished yet! Even though she is still in the process of finding healing from the abuse and freedom from her addiction, she understands that God is at work in her life. Our most recent talk was filled with hope: "I do believe that I can break free, even though it will be difficult. I feel like God is staying with me through this and can help me overcome it." Amen! Don't give up, sister.

I share McKenna's story because she explains so well what happens when we allow shame to take over. It's as if shame closes our ears to God's forgiving voice but gives full volume to the Enemy's condemning lies. Are you familiar with

Satan's lies? Sheesh. I am! "You're too sinful, Jessie. God could never love a hypocrite like you. You're so far gone, you might as well just keep on sinning." Yeah, I know all about his lies. Ephesians 6:11 warns us to put on God's spiritual armor so we can understand and stand firm against Satan's strategies. Well, here's one military strategy we should definitely be aware of: Satan's arsenal includes excessive shame. He wants you to drown in it. He wants you to believe you're alone in your shame, because if you think that way, you won't get help. (Side note: Satan also tries to use shame to *get* us to sin. Have you ever felt embarrassed, left out, or too uptight because you didn't want to do what "everybody else" was doing? That's unwarranted shame in action!)

If you're convinced that no one will understand, everyone will think less of you, or others will shun you if you come clean about your sin, let's just say there's not a whole lot of motivation to be open about it! Who's out looking for abject humiliation? Me neither. So we go on trying to do this solo sin-slayer thing, which doesn't work very well (as you may have found). Satan may be damned, but he's no dummy! He knows that just as there is strength in numbers, there is weakness in isolation. And shame pushes us to isolate ourselves from potential help.

Second reason Satan loves shame: It simultaneously starves truth and feeds bondage. When we allow shame to rule our hearts, we become spiritually anemic and vulnerable to Satan's attacks. Put another way? Shame is like cancer. Did you know that cancer cells steal nutrients from healthy cells? Cancer cells eat up the fuel intended for the rest of the body, causing the healthy cells to starve. As the healthy cells get weaker, some cancers then attack the organs and, if not treated, can eventually kill the person.

Shame is like that. A girl's shame eats up the spiritual nourishment meant for her body, leaving her weak and vulnerable. All her energy is spent just trying to survive, trying to cope. The shame attacks her healthy "organs"—her heart, mind, and relationship with God. If the shame isn't treated, she might even die—a slow, numbing, spiritual death. Shame's cancer-like nature explains how even a spiritually healthy Christian girl can eventually "starve" to death from unconfessed, secret sin. And that's why I'm so passionate about rooting out unhealthy shame! I don't want to see you die; I want to see you *thrive*.

Shame keeps us from getting help. It starves truth and feeds bondage (like cancer). But there's a third reason Satan loves shame: It actually perpetuates addiction. The words I shared earlier from McKenna touched on this. When we feel so ashamed and down and defeated that we can't imagine ever breaking free, we lose the motivation to try. We start rationalizing our sin—giving up and giving in. We sin. We're ashamed. We feel defeated, so we sin again. Shame is that spin factor on the sin cycle that keeps you whirling around like a crazy top!

For all three of these reasons, shame has got to go. Now, remember, I'm not saying we should ignore our conscience. We should feel badly when we sin! But there is a place to take that sorrow, and it's called the Cross. (In chapter 7, we're going to spend some more time talking about healthy regret and godly sorrow.)

# The Antidote to Shame

Good news: There *is* an antidote to shame! But before I share that secret, I need you to do something for me. I want you to take a look at Psalm 34. By the time this book is over, you're probably going to be sick of hearing me talk about it. It's my favorite psalm on the topic of pain and sin and God and growth and prayer and contentment and praise—oh yeah, and shame. So why don't the two of you get acquainted? Even though I'd prefer you read it in your own Bible (so you can highlight and make notes to your heart's content), I'm going to print the whole thing here in case you don't have a Bible handy. Enjoy!

> ¹I will praise the LORD at all times.
>   I will constantly speak his praises.
> ²I will boast only in the LORD;
>   let all who are helpless take heart.
> ³Come, let us tell of the LORD's greatness;
>   let us exalt his name together.
>
> ⁴I prayed to the LORD, and he answered me.
>   He freed me from all my fears.
> ⁵Those who look to him for help will be radiant with joy;
>   no shadow of shame will darken their faces.
> ⁶In my desperation I prayed, and the LORD listened;
>   he saved me from all my troubles.

⁷For the angel of the LORD is a guard;
    he surrounds and defends all who fear him.

⁸Taste and see that the LORD is good.
    Oh, the joys of those who take refuge in him!
⁹Fear the LORD, you his godly people,
    for those who fear him will have all they need.
¹⁰Even strong young lions sometimes grow hungry,
    but those who trust in the LORD will lack no
      good thing.

¹¹Come, my children, and listen to me,
    and I will teach you to fear the LORD.
¹²Does anyone want to live a life
    that is long and prosperous?
¹³Then keep your tongue from speaking evil
    and your lips from telling lies!
¹⁴Turn away from evil and do good.
    Search for peace, and work to maintain it.

¹⁵The eyes of the LORD watch over those who do right;
    his ears are open to their cries for help.
¹⁶But the LORD turns his face against those who do evil;
    he will erase their memory from the earth.
¹⁷The LORD hears his people when they call to him
      for help.
    He rescues them from all their troubles.
¹⁸The LORD is close to the brokenhearted;
    he rescues those whose spirits are crushed.

¹⁹The righteous person faces many troubles,
   but the LORD comes to rescue each time.
²⁰For the LORD protects the bones of the righteous;
   not one of them is broken!

²¹Calamity will surely overtake the wicked,
   and those who hate the righteous will be punished.
²²But the LORD will redeem those who serve him.
   No one who takes refuge in him will be condemned.

Great psalm, right?

Okay, I promised to let you in on the antidote to shame, so let's get to it. Take another look at verse 5:

Those who look to him for help will be radiant with joy;
   no shadow of shame will darken their faces.

What is the antidote to shame? *Look to God.* Don't accuse me of being overly simplistic just yet! There's a lot of good stuff packed into those three little words. The Hebrew verb *nabat*, translated "look at" or "look to," means more than gazing up at the sky toward heaven wishing for a miracle. *Nabat* means to show regard for, pay attention to, or consider.⁷ Don't let the simplicity of that sentence numb you to the truth wrapped up in it. The girl who is willing to honor God, pay close attention to Him and His Word, and keep Him in mind throughout every decision and every circumstance is "radiant with joy." She *shines*. I *love* that! This psalm promises that the girl who turns to God for help with her secret sin won't be disappointed. No shadow of shame will darken her face (in the Hebrew, her "face" meaning her "presence") if she is willing to embrace His love, savor His forgiveness, and follow His guidance.

Can you imagine what it would be like to be free of shame? Shame certainly has a way of "darkening" life, doesn't it? Maybe it's been so long since you *didn't* struggle with a secret sin that you can't even remember how bright and vibrant life was before shame entered the picture. If so, let me refresh your memory: A girl who isn't darkened by shame has the freedom to be herself. She doesn't feel the pressure to keep up appearances or hide the truth from others. A girl who is radiant with joy brings life to those around her and offers grace at every turn. She smiles, enjoys helping others, and has hope for the future. A girl who is radiant with joy trusts God, believes God, follows God, and honors God. Know anyone like that? If you do, then you know that those kinds of girls are a joy to be around. Do *you* want to be like that? If so, then look to God.

How? How can you look to God when you can't physically see Him? We said earlier that looking to God means to show regard for God, to pay attention to or consider Him. Psalm 34 gives some practical ways we can do just that. We can look to God by:

- Praising Him—constantly!—for who He is, for what He has done, and even for what He's going to do (verses 1-3)
- Talking to Him in prayer (verse 4)

- Fearing Him, which means respecting Him (verse 9)—taking His instructions to heart, seeing Him in the world around us, and getting excited to share Him with others
- Trusting Him with our lives, which includes our circumstances (verse 10)
- Telling the truth (verse 13)
- Turning from evil and doing good instead (verses 14, 19-20)
- Trying to be at peace with others (verse 14)
- Calling to Him for help first (instead of to our friends, our boyfriends, or even the Internet) (verse 17)
- Serving Him by serving others (verse 22)

And that's just from one psalm! The Bible has lots more to say about turning to God. As you study His Word, you'll see more connections between looking to God and kicking shame to the curb.

Look, I know that you might be so entrenched in sin that "looking to God" sounds at best like a Sunday-school answer and at worst like you just wasted your money on this book! Can getting rid of shame really be that simple? Well, yes and no. Remember, this is a journey, not a three-step process. Understanding and putting into practice that list from Psalm 34 isn't going to happen by the weekend. But trust me, God knows how to mend us because He's the one who made us! If He tells us that looking to Him will rid us of shame, that's where we're going to begin. As for practical advice on *how* to regard God, break a cycle of addiction, and so on, don't worry—we'll get there, too.

So what do you think? Are you tired of the sin-shame-despair cycle? God *wants* you to be radiant with joy. He wants you to look to Him so that His light can chase away those shadows of shame. It's *His* light that reflects off our unashamed faces, making us radiate joy. But He is always the gentleman. He'll never force you to turn to Him, even if He knows that His love and His ways are in your best interest. He wants you to *choose* Him, freely, all on your own. Will you do that with me now?

*Father God, I need You. It's pretty obvious I can't do this on my own! Shame has been eating away at me, stealing my joy and darkening my world. I'm scared to come clean, but I know I can trust You. So I'm turning to You today—right now—because I know You're the only One who can help me find true freedom. Free me! Free me from my sin and shame. Give me the strength to begin this journey of healing. Amen.*

## Discussion Questions

1. *Are you a silent sufferer? Do you know any other girls who struggle with sins they're ashamed of?*

2. *Why do you think it's so hard for us girls to come clean about our sins and get help?*

3. *Is shame ever a good thing? Why or why not?*

4. *What are some reasons Satan loves to use excessive shame as a weapon against us?*

5. *What lies does Satan use to keep you personally from being open and honest about your sin?*

6. *Psalm 34:5 says that those who look to God are "radiant" and won't be darkened by shame. What does it mean to look to God? What are some practical ways you can do that?*

## CHAPTER 2

# What's Your Secret?

You are one of a kind. No one else has the same thumbprint, personality, or memories. So it'd be ridiculous to assume that we all struggle with the same sins for the same reasons. But there are similarities to our struggles, and understanding those common threads can help us see that we're not alone. We're all in this together!

Before we talk more about the similarities, though, let's talk about the "secret sins" themselves. Again, these aren't one-size-fits-all sins. You might be struggling with something I don't even mention here, but that doesn't make it any less serious. It's also quite common to wrestle with more than one of these sins at the same time. The reason I want to go through them one by one is because they *are* different in some ways, and I want to explain what God thinks about each one and some info that maybe you haven't considered before.

I also want to explain why I've chosen these five sins instead of the gazillion other ones out there—sins such as lying, jealousy, stealing, and hatred. The sins we're going to talk about in this book aren't necessarily worse, dirtier, or harder to ditch than other sins. (God says that *every* sin is serious!) But even though all sin is equal (because it separates us from God), some sins are more hefty than others because they have more serious consequences. These five sins fit that category; they're more dangerous because they have bigger natural consequences. I also picked these five sins because more and more girls are struggling with them (while thinking they're the only ones who do!). If I don't specifically address your secret sin in this chapter, please don't tune out. The rest of what we're going to talk about—how to see sin, deal with it, and move on—applies to every sin, big or small. (Plus, you never know whether a girl right next to you *is* struggling with one of these sins and could use your understanding and support.)

One more thing before I give you the lineup: Be wise, sis. If you know that reading even a matter-of-fact description of a sin might cause you to be more tempted to sin or to try a sin for the first time, *please* just skip to page 33. The last thing in the world I want to do is lead you into danger! There's wisdom in knowing your limits.

Common Secret Sins

# Cutting

---

### DESCRIPTION

The "experts" call it non-suicidal self-injury (NSSI), but you probably know this secret sin as *cutting*. Despite that name, NSSI isn't limited to actual cutting. It could be any act someone performs to purposefully hurt themselves without trying to commit suicide. It doesn't matter whether it's biting, burning, slicing, inserting, picking at, hitting, or swallowing. If it hurts and it's done on purpose, that's NSSI. I'll refer to NSSI as *cutting* for the rest of this book, just to keep it simple.

### GOD'S TAKE

You might be surprised to know just how often the Bible mentions cutting. It's definitely not a new phenomenon. In Old Testament times, people cut themselves in times of great mourning (see Jeremiah 16:6; 48:37; Micah 5:1 [HCSB]), as part of idolatrous worship (see 1 Kings 18:28), and as self-flagellation (which is a fancy way of saying they hurt themselves to try to prove their religious devotion; see Jeremiah 41:5). In the New Testament, we read about a demon-possessed man who "wandered among the burial caves and in the hills, howling and cutting himself with sharp stones" (Mark 5:2-5).

It's probably not a huge surprise that God doesn't want us to hurt ourselves for *any* reason. In the Old Testament, He specifically forbade His chosen people, the Israelites, from cutting themselves as a coping mechanism when someone they loved died (see Leviticus 19:28; Deuteronomy 14:1). As for our demon-possessed brother from Mark 5, once Jesus got hold of his life, the man got dressed and rejoined society, so I think it's safe to assume he quit cutting (along with howling, for which his neighbors were especially thankful).

Peter, one of Jesus' closest friends and disciples, said that Jesus "personally carried our sins in his body on the cross so that we [could] be dead to sin and live for what is right. By *his wounds* you are healed" (1 Peter 2:24, emphasis added). And if we're healed by Jesus' wounds, there's no reason for us to inflict our own any longer!

### WHY CUTTING IS SO TEMPTING

I don't know a single girl who cuts because she's worshiping Baal or demon-possessed. (Not saying it couldn't happen, but I doubt those are *your* reasons if this is your secret sin.) Mourning, on the other hand, seems more connected with modern-day reasons. Why is it tempting? Cutting seems like a way to cope with extreme pain, pressure, anxiety, and hopelessness— emotions girls in the twenty-first century know all too much about. There might be scientific reasons for the temptation too. Some evidence suggests that the same part of your brain that handles emotional pain also handles physical pain.[1] Regardless of what science says, girls' experiences clearly show that—for whatever reason—physically hurting themselves *does* ease emotional pain for a split second in time. And when you feel as though you're drowning or imploding or ready to die, that brief second of relief or control can sound mighty tempting. Unfortunately, that short moment of release leaves two scars: one on the skin and one on the heart, both of them permanent reminders.

**THINGS TO CONSIDER**

Every cutter I've met completely understood that "seeing red" (making herself bleed) did not get to the root of her pain. In fact, many girls have said that cutting makes the pain worse in the long run and requires deeper and deeper cuts to feel "relief." Lesson? If you've never cut, don't start now! Once you start any addictive behavior, it is incredibly difficult to stop. In chapter 6, we'll talk more about the nature of addictions and how to overcome them.

# Substance Abuse

**DESCRIPTION**

Substance abuse is the "excessive use of a potentially addictive substance, especially one that may modify body functions, such as alcohol and drugs."[2] From "skunk" to a cigarette, from vodka to Vicodin—if you excessively swallow, smoke, snort, or inject it to escape from reality (illegally or not), you're abusing a substance.

**GOD'S TAKE**

The only "substance" the Bible refers to is alcohol, but what God has to say about wine[3] and getting drunk applies to any substance a modern-day chemical chef can cook up.

Ever heard of Proverbs 31? You know, that passage that tells us what a godly woman looks like? Well, right before King Lemuel's mother gives her son that great piece of advice on how to choose a bride, she tells him why he shouldn't drink. Here's what the Queen Mother had to say:

> It is not for kings, O Lemuel, to guzzle wine.
> Rulers should not crave alcohol.

> For if they drink, they may forget the law
>> and not give justice to the oppressed.
> Alcohol is for the dying,
>> and wine for those in bitter distress.
> Let them drink to forget their poverty
>> and remember their troubles no more.

PROVERBS 31:4-7

Now, maybe you're thinking, *Wait a minute. I am in "bitter distress"! Does that mean it's okay for me to drink if I'm just trying to "remember [my] troubles no more"?* Nice try. See, if we are God's children and He's the King, then spiritually speaking, we are royalty. We have no excuse to drown away our sorrows with alcohol or any other substance because we *aren't* just common folk going about our daily grind with no hope for the future (see Jeremiah 29:11). The Ultimate King has purchased us, redeemed us, and now counts us as His daughters. If we have placed our faith in Christ, He has given us a hope and a future. We should find our comfort in Him and in His Word, not in a pill or bottle.

Paul sums it up pretty clearly in Ephesians 5:18: "Don't be drunk with wine, because that will ruin your life." Substance abuse = ruined life. Duly noted. He goes on to give an alternative—a better "mood-altering" substance (person): "Be filled with the Holy Spirit." If you've placed your faith in Jesus Christ, then God has given you His very *Spirit!* The great I AM within you is more than enough to cope with any circumstance.

## WHY SUBSTANCE ABUSE IS SO TEMPTING

When we're not remaining in Christ (more on that in chapter 3), life can sometimes feel out of control. When you're an emotional mess, drinking, swallowing, or smoking something that will take away the pain ASAP starts to look mighty tempting.

### THINGS TO CONSIDER
Paul wasn't joking when he said that substance abuse ruins your life. Even if you feel as if you've got your intake monitored and under control, don't underestimate the way mood-altering substances can destroy your body and heart. Proverbs 23:29-35 paints a sobering picture (no pun intended) of substance abusers. They basically bring a whole lot of pain on themselves! Unnecessary anguish, sorrow, fights, bruises, bloodshot eyes, hallucinations, and an addiction that is very hard to quit are definitely not worth the temporary pleasure of that drink or drug.

# Eating Disorders

### DESCRIPTION
An eating disorder is a state of mind that affects a person's normal relationship with food. Eating disorders include everything from anorexia (not eating) to binge-eating disorder (eating too much). Two other common eating disorders among girls are bulimia (eating and then purging by vomiting) and exercise bulimia (eating and then purging through excessive exercise). There are others, but we're going to focus on those four in this book.

### GOD'S TAKE
In Philippians 3:18-19, Paul tearfully warned the Philippian church, "There are many whose conduct shows they are really enemies of the cross of Christ. They are headed for destruction. Their god is their appetite . . . and they think only about this life here on earth." Other translations

read, "Their god is their stomach" or "Their god is their belly." Whether you're focused on eating too much or too little, if you're focused on food period, you've got an idol problem. Focusing on food and our weight is thinking "only about this life here on earth." God wants us to be so much more than that! You are more than a number on a scale, and you are more than what you've eaten today.

God is way more concerned with the attitudes inside our hearts than with the food we put in our mouths. That was the point of a parable Jesus told some religious types in Matthew 15 who were über-preoccupied with which foods they could and couldn't eat based on the Levitical (think "Old Testament") laws. He said,

> It's not what goes into your mouth that defiles you; you are defiled by the words that come out of your mouth. . . .
>
> Anything you eat passes through the stomach and then goes into the sewer. But the words you speak come from the heart—that's what defiles you. For from the heart come evil thoughts, murder, adultery, all sexual immorality, theft, lying, and slander. These are what defile you.
> MATTHEW 15:11,17-20

In other words, it's not about the food we do or don't eat; it's about our heart attitudes. God hates eating disorders because they reveal wrong heart attitudes about food, body image, and ultimately Him. We should do everything—including eating—for God's glory (see 1 Corinthians 10:31). With an eating disorder, we eat for *our* glory (so we'll be "more beautiful"). Or we eat to numb pain with pleasure, which in essence tells God, "You aren't enough for me. I need food to fill a void You can't touch."

## WHY EATING DISORDERS ARE SO TEMPTING

Interesting, isn't it? The crazy rise in eating disorders over the past fifty years just happens to follow the crazy rise in media and advertising over the same time period.[4] Eating disorders are so tempting partly because we're faced with images of "perfection" every single cotton-pickin' place we look. It's exhausting! And many of us think that the easiest way to get the image of perfection is to starve ourselves of food or purge it once we've eaten it. (I was one of those girls, by the way. Because I couldn't make myself throw up—go figure—I resorted to exercise bulimia for a number of years. Thankfully, God taught me a better way to view my body and food, and I have been free from that secret sin for more than a decade.)

At the same time, convenience foods have become a huge market. We are too busy to eat healthful food, which would give us fuel *and* a healthy-looking body. Instead we eat junk and then feel miserable about it.

## THINGS TO CONSIDER

When God created food—of the healthy, plant variety— He said that it was good (see Genesis 1:12). He gave us "every seed-bearing plant throughout the earth and all the fruit trees for [our] food" (verse 29). We can't let ourselves spurn as "bad" something that God says is "good" (see Acts 10:9-15 for Peter's spiritual lesson about that)!

God has a lot to say about your body, and none of it is negative. He designed you with purpose and expertise like a master craftsman (see Psalm 139:13-16), and He's proud of His handiwork. He doesn't want you messing with the mold He used *on purpose*; He wants you to honor Him with that marvelous body He has given you (see 1 Corinthians 6:20).

*Shameless Plug: I'm really passionate about how you view your body and your relationship with food. If you don't realize just how beautiful you are or if you just want to explore more about a healthy, God-honoring view of food and health, check out the next LIFE, LOVE & GOD book,* Backwards Beauty: How to Feel Ugly in 10 Simple Steps.

# Sexual Sin

### DESCRIPTION

There's a whole lot of sexual sin out there. For this book, I'm going to narrow it down to the most common for girls: having sex before you're married, masturbation (alone or "making out" with a boyfriend), and pornography (pictures or in story form). I will address homosexuality in the next section, although it would fit here as well.

### GOD'S TAKE

God's design for sex: one man and one woman within marriage. Any sexual act outside the boundary of marriage is sin: "solo" sex, oral sex, sex with your boyfriend, looking at pictures of (or reading about) other people having sex. You get the idea.

Hebrews 13:4 says,

> Marriage must be respected by all, and the marriage bed kept undefiled, because God will judge immoral people and adulterers. (HCSB)

Is God some killjoy in the sky who wants to keep you from enjoying the pleasure of sex? No way! He designed sex, and He knows that the greatest pleasure comes when sex is kept where He intended it to be kept. He's not out to keep you from pleasure; He wants your pleasure to be heightened. He knows that when we ignore His plan for sex and do things our way, we won't experience the full potential of pleasure. We'll also pay a price—emotionally and sometimes even physically. That's why He warns us to R-U-N from sexual sin (see 1 Corinthians 6:18).

> ***Shameless Plug Numero Dos: If you want to dive deeper into this idea of purity, why you should wait for sex (and what to do if you haven't), plus learn the secrets of a God-honoring relationship, check out the first LIFE, LOVE & GOD book,*** **Crushed: Why Guys Don't Have to Make or Break You.**

### WHY SEXUAL SIN IS SO TEMPTING

Let's be real here: Sexual sin is tempting because it feels good. But it feels good in different ways. The physical pleasure of an orgasm makes sex or masturbation tempting, sure. But as girls, we also crave love and have a deep desire *to be desired*. It's that longing for emotional intimacy (as well as reading romance novels and watching romantic movies) that often makes a physical relationship with a guy so tempting. But when we value being loved by a guy more than we value being holy in God's sight—voilà!—we've created an idol in our hearts.

### THINGS TO CONSIDER

When it comes to sex, God made humans way more complex than animals. He designed us not to just make babies but also to be "united into one" (Genesis 2:24). Paul explains in 1 Corinthians 6:16,

> There's more to sex than mere skin on skin. Sex is as much spiritual mystery as physical fact. As written in Scripture, "The two become one." (MSG)

A man and woman "become one" by the act of physical intimacy. Sex solidifies people. It's like relationship cement. God designed sexual intimacy to join together two people, but He intends the cement to be laid after the commitment of marriage.

Although masturbation or pornography doesn't always cement you to another individual (there are instances where it can), it still departs from God's design of "one man and one woman within marriage." It might seem like a lesser evil than actually having sex, but God doesn't call us to betterness; He calls us to holiness (see 1 Peter 1:16).

## Same-Sex Relationships

### DESCRIPTION

First, same-sex relationships are not the same as same-sex attraction (or SSA). Being tempted to sin is not the same as sinning. In other words, SSA isn't wrong unless you act on that attraction by entering into a relationship with, getting physical with, or lusting after a person of the same gender. In fact, there are a growing number of believers who struggle with SSA but who have chosen not to act on their attraction because they believe that the Bible says homosexuality is wrong. I admire their courage and commitment to God's standard of holiness!

## GOD'S TAKE

If you struggle with SSA, whether you've acted on your attraction or not, you've probably already heard at least some of the Bible verses that address homosexuality. You may have (though I hope not!) had those verses hurled at you like grenades from behind a holier-than-thou fortress. If you've been hurt by others' interpretations of those verses (even if they were technically right), I'm truly sorry. Before I give you God's take, please know that I am neither a grenade thrower nor a Pharisee. I *am* a student of Scripture, though, and sometimes what I see in Scripture is right and true and holy and *still* breaks my heart.

See, from my study of Scripture, it is clear to me that God's best and perfect plan for you does not include a homosexual lifestyle. At the very beginning, God made a woman for Adam and explained the plan: marriage = one man + one woman + one lifetime. Genesis 2:24 explains, "A *man* leaves his father and mother and bonds with his *wife*, and they become one flesh"[5] (HCSB, emphasis added). After studying every passage of Scripture that handles the lesbian, gay, bisexual, and transgender (LGBT) issue from both sides of the fence, I am more convinced than ever that God doesn't want us to have same-sex relationships. But because of personal conversations I've had with LGBTs, I'm also more convinced than ever that SSA is a complex, lonely, often-misunderstood issue that deserves more than pat "church answers." Homosexuality isn't just a theological issue to be studied; it involves people with stories, complexities, and desires that may never be realized. I get that. I *feel* that.

I wish I could explain in a simple, straightforward way *why* God condemns homosexuality. I really do. If we were going to play devil's advocate, it's hard to understand why a God of love wouldn't give His blessing to anyone showing love to another human being. I do think I see some of His reasons (kind of similar to His reasons for putting boundaries on heterosexual relationships), but I'm also just a puny human trying to get inside the mind of an infinite God! I can't always understand, so I trust. I trust that if He says that same-sex relationships aren't right, He has a very good reason why. And I also trust that He will give you strength for each day as you figure out how to love and obey Him with your whole heart, even if your feelings and attractions tug hard at it.

### WHY SAME-SEX RELATIONSHIPS ARE SO TEMPTING

Girls are tempted by same-sex relationships for different reasons. Some have been deeply hurt by one or more men in their lives. Others are convinced that being a boy is better than being a girl, so they take on masculine personas. Others simply crave love and acceptance so deeply that they'd rather be desired by another girl than not at all. And some girls can't point to any trauma or abnormal experience to explain their feelings; they just have them.

### THINGS TO CONSIDER

If you struggle with SSA and aren't exactly sure what the Bible says about homosexuality, make it a priority to find out. If you're not sure where to begin in that study, you could start by browsing the resources at www.LifeLoveandGod.com/unashamed. If you don't struggle with SSA, please also study God's Word, leaving room in your heart to extend genuine grace and love to those struggling with SSA or who are in homosexual relationships. Jesus didn't shy away from people, period; He didn't care what category their sin fell into. You and I follow in His footsteps when we offer a compassionate voice of truth.

# Five Peas in a Pod

Now that we have a point of reference for the five main kinds of sins we are hiding in our closets, let's get back to looking at some similarities. No matter how unique your sin or your reasons for sinning, there are some aspects common with other silent sufferers. We talked about the first common denominator in chapter 1: shame. (Five-second recap: Unhealthy shame keeps us from getting help, starves truth, feeds bondage, and perpetuates addiction. But the antidote to unhealthy shame is to look to God.) I want to throw six more common threads out there for you to consider.

## They're Secret

Because each of these sins usually carries a two-liter of shame along with it, very few girls feel they can share their struggles with anyone else. The secrecy surrounding these sins keeps us in bondage because we have no accountability, help, or support from people who love and care about us.

## They're Common

Even though you might feel as though you're the only one who struggles with a particular sin, you're not. Our hush-hush attitude about our sins has hidden the truth that they're surprisingly common—not only common in the sense that a lot of girls struggle with them but also common in the sense of "nothing new." The temptations we face now, in the twenty-first century, are the same temptations people faced three thousand years ago. Certain sins (such as porn) are more in-your-face available since the technology age, but the root temptations are the same.

> The temptations in your life are no different from what others experience. And God is faithful. He will not allow the temptation to be more than you can stand. When you are tempted, he will show you a way out so that you can endure.
>
> I CORINTHIANS 10:13

God knows all hearts, and He knows just how common every sin is. Not only that, but He promises to give a way out of every sin, including the secret ones.

## They're Against Ourselves

One of the warnings Paul gave the Corinthian church about sexual sin was that it is a sin against our own bodies. I've always thought that was interesting. But as I thought about each of the five secret sins in that lineup, guess what? Cutting is against your body. Substance abuse is against your body. Eating disorders are against your body. Even homosexual relationships are sins against your own body.

So what? Why is it a big deal if you sin against your own body? Logically, wouldn't it be worse to sin against others? What I do to my body is my business, right? Well, for starters, it's just dumb. (Am I allowed to say that?) I mean, you're stuck in this body for as many years as God gives you breath, so it would be on the smart side to take care of it. (Anybody here want to lose the ability to have kids from an eating disorder or get cancer because of a sexually transmitted disease? Not so much.) But in 1 Corinthians 6:18-20, Paul gives another reason why sins against our own body are especially unwise:

> Sexual immorality [or cutting, or substance abuse, and so on] is a sin against your own body. Don't you realize that your body is the temple of the Holy Spirit, who lives in you and was given to you by God? You do not belong to yourself, for God bought you with a high price. So you must honor God with your body.

Our bodies aren't our own at all. God bought them with the price of His Son, and now we belong to Him. Part of following Christ means handing over the deed to your life. The term *Christian* (Greek *Christianos*) literally means "belonging to Christ."[6]

But sins against our bodies are disrespectful to God not only because He owns them but also because those sins vandalize His temple. Quick history lesson: In the Old Testament, God chose to dwell with His people in a special building (first in the tabernacle, then in a series of temples that were built and then torn down by conquerors). Then Jesus came. He explained that God was going to do something a little—make that a lot—different when it came to dwelling with His people. Forty days after Jesus' resurrection, that revolutionary new way of dwelling arrived: the Holy Spirit.

God's temple 2.0 is *your body*.

This is crazy stuff when you really stop to think about

it. If you are a Christian, the Holy Spirit lives in you. So when you sin against your body, it's as though you're taking a can of spray paint to God's holy temple. And, as you can imagine, God doesn't take too kindly to His children's tagging up His joint. That would be like your three-year-old little sister taking a permanent marker to your bed, shelves, and antique piggy bank. (True story. And I certainly didn't take too kindly to that either, although she was so darn cute with her blonde hair and chubby cheeks that it was hard to be mad for too long.)

Secret sins are serious business for a lot of reasons, but would you agree that defacing God's property/holy temple might top the list?

## They're Addictive

As you've probably experienced, each of these secret sins can become an addiction at lightning speed. The addiction factor can keep us trapped in a sin despite our best efforts. Sorry to keep teasing you on this one, but you're going to have to wait until chapter 6 for more on this topic!

## They're Rooted in Coping or Craving

Another common thread between secret sins is that we do them for one of only two reasons: to *cope* (with strong emotions, crazy circumstances) or to satisfy a *craving* for something (love, pleasure).

Another of my "little sisters," Leah, articulates what so many girls feel. When I asked her why she used to cut, she shared,

My home life was so chaotic, unsafe, painful, and insecure. I was incredibly broken, full of shame and anger, and had a whole bunch of emotions I wasn't quite sure what to do with. I felt at the time that cutting was the one thing in my life I could control. I controlled when I did it, where I did it, and how I did it.

Can you relate? Cutting, substance abuse, and sometimes even eating disorders make a girl feel as if she's in control of her life or at least give her brief relief from feeling as though she's drowning. They are a way to cope. Is sin the right way to deal with intense emotions? No. And most of us know that, even if we act otherwise. What we don't usually realize, though, is that our actions essentially say to God, "You are not enough for me. You're not big enough or strong enough to help me deal with my emotions, so I'm going to have to find a way to deal with them on my own."

Coping's evil twin is *craving*. A craving is a powerful desire for something. We might crave chocolate, pizza, or (my favorite) black-raspberry chocolate-chip gelato. In the world of secret sins, those cravings come in different forms. We crave love from our boyfriend, so we go too far with him. We crave others' admiration for a hot body, so we starve ourselves to get "the look" and their envy. We crave the pleasure of sex, so we masturbate. Are those the right ways to get what we want? Of course not. And most of us know that too. Again, what we don't usually realize is that our actions essentially say to God, "You are not enough for me. I desire other things more than I desire You, and I'm willing to set our relationship aside to satisfy my craving."

Pretty heavy stuff when we think about it that way, huh?

Think about your secret sins. When you sin, are you trying to cope with strong emotions such as pain, regret, anger, and fear? Or do you sin to satisfy a craving for something that you feel you just *have* to have to be happy? The answer to that question is going to determine how you combat that sin.

## They Trick and Harden Us

This common characteristic of every sin should—how do I put this?—scare the tar out of you (in a good way, of course).

Sin can appear as harmless as a fluffy-tailed squirrel, but if you give in to the temptation to pet it, it will bite with the tenacity of a mini Tasmanian devil. (Another true story—both about sin and about the squirrel. Yeah, I don't know why I thought it would be a good idea to feed that squirrel some of my bagel, but I digress). Sin is deceptive. Hebrews 3:13 says,

> You must warn each other every day, while it is still
> "today," so that none of you will be deceived by sin
> and hardened against God.

Chances are you've already experienced the dark side of a sin that seemed harmless, but this verse also warns us that continuing in sin has dire consequences. Sin continues to harden your heart toward God until you eventually get to the point where you don't care whether you sin or not.

And that's a place you never ever want to end up. Apathy toward sin is extremely dangerous. It can kill you stone-dead spiritually.

Secret sins trick you and then dry you out, harden you up, leave you stale and tasteless. And it can happen faster than you might imagine. But there's good news, remember?

> Those who look to him for help will be radiant with joy;
> no shadow of shame will darken their faces.
>
> PSALM 34:5

Secret sins might have a lot of negative things in common, but at the end of the day, they're all just sin—plain old rebellion-against-God, been-happening-since-the-Fall S-I-N. No matter what sin you're trapped in, sin is sin. And the good news for you and for me is that God is in the business of taking our sin, forgiving it, and then chucking it from one end of the sky to the other (see Psalm 103:12). We've got a whole lot more to chew on regarding the nature of sin and the beauty of God's forgiveness, but first will you pray with me?

> *Heavenly God, thank You for reminding me that I'm not alone in my hurt or in my sin. Sometimes I forget that I'm not the only one who feels as if she's sinking. So even though I'm still on this journey toward healing, I pray for all the other girls struggling like I am. Help them find freedom, God. Show us how to band together and fight these things as a sisterhood because there's strength in togetherness. I love You. Amen.*

# Discussion Questions

1. Do you struggle (or have you struggled) with any of the sins mentioned in this chapter? If so, which ones?

2. What does God's Word have to say specifically about those sins?

3. Did you learn anything new about secret sin? What in this chapter surprised you?

4. Why is it a big deal to commit sin against your own body?

5. Is the secret sin you struggle with a way to cope or a craving? Why do you think it's important to know the difference?

6. Do you think your heart is in danger of getting hard toward God because of your sin? Why or why not?

## MADISON'S STORY

The secret sin I struggled with was my feelings for another girl. I grew up a Christian and knew the Bible said homosexuality was a sin. When I started developing feelings for Danae, a good friend of mine who was bisexual at the time, I was very confused. I didn't want to have those feelings. I wanted to obey God.

Nothing happened between us for a few months, but one night I confessed to our group of friends that I had feelings for her. She was in shock and then confessed that she, too, had feelings for me. A weird sense of relief came over me. Everyone wants to be known and loved, and knowing that someone felt that way about me was like a puzzle piece being snapped into place.

My gut was telling me to run away, but I had this deep craving and longing for love and for someone to be crazy about me. I didn't care that she was a girl. For the next few months, I struggled, going back and forth between doing what I knew was right and doing what I *thought* could be the path for me. I started to rationalize my feelings and deny the truth of the Bible. Danae showered me with love—bought me jewelry, gave me flowers, and sacrificed her time to be with me. I started to lie to my parents, to my Christian friends, to God, and to myself. I kept telling myself that liking a girl couldn't be a sin because it was making me happy. My sin was clouding my judgment, my decisions, and my faith. I wanted to live in my sin and also keep my relationship with God. But though God is a loving God, He is also a righteous God, and my sin tore us apart.

I wanted to be with Danae and thought that we were

meant to be together. However, the Holy Spirit was always talking to me. When I felt guilty, I would get sad, but then I'd manipulate my thoughts. I became selfish and wanted things to work out in my favor. I ignored the fact that my relationship with Danae was not healthy. She became my idol. I relied on her for my happiness and my confidence. I got mad at God, that He would consider something like this a sin. I thought I was happy, but my sin was confusing everything.

Sometimes we can't fight battles on our own. I'm thankful that God intervened by having my parents find out about my secret sin. I will never forget that night. My parents' reaction—disappointment mixed with anger—hit me hard. I didn't expect people who love me unconditionally to respond that way, but their reaction shook me, woke me up, dragged me out of that dark tunnel, and broke the vines that were slowly strangling my life. My parents said I had two choices: (1) move out and live with Danae, in which case they would cut my education funding and cut me out of their lives, or (2) break up with her. I had to choose between throwing my whole life away by keeping Danae or keeping the rest of my life and mending it back together.

I wanted to die that night. But I chose to keep my life.

My heart was crushed. I cried until I had no tears left inside me, but something happened that night. Though I felt like I had nothing, like everything had been stripped away, I gained my faith back. I felt His grace. It felt real. All of a sudden, I felt as if I had been this prisoner on a ship with no water to drink. Once I saw the light again, I could taste and see that God is good!

When I was in the middle of it all, I felt like I was the only one who struggled with this sin. I remember going to church every Sunday and feeling conflicted. I wondered what people would think about me if they found out. I knew that Christians should be loving and forgiving, but I felt like I would be shunned if they found out about my sin. If a relationship with another girl is your secret sin, know that you are not alone. Know that God is bigger than your sin. Isaiah 59:1-2 says, "Listen! The LORD's arm is not too weak to save you, nor is his ear too deaf to hear you call. It's your sins that have cut you off from God." Pray for help. Pray for support. Pray for clarity. Keep fighting.

If you have a friend who has chosen this sin, be there for her. Help your friends who are struggling. I had one Christian friend who fought to help me see what I was getting myself into. Even though I didn't listen to her at the time, I realize now that she was being a true friend. Don't judge; just listen and pray. Galatians 6:1 says,

> If another believer is overcome by some sin,
> you who are godly should gently and humbly
> help that person back onto the right path.

From this experience, I've grown to have a deeper understanding of who God is. I have learned to take ownership of my relationship with Him. I understand what grace is and how thankful I am for Jesus and that He died on the cross for that sin. I deserved to die! But God is a merciful God. I am thankful that although I sank into depression after the breakup, I regained my faith over time, and slowly God blessed me for my obedience and gave me a new life, a life worth living, a life for Him.

# CHAPTER 3

# The Disconnect

I'll never forget the day I bought my first car. It didn't matter that my new Toyota MR2 was almost fifteen years old, had only two seats, looked like a giant origami airplane, and was painted gold; that car was mine. It had four wheels, and with them I could go where I pleased when I pleased with whom I pleased. In a word, that rusting little sports car spelled freedom.

I bought the MR2 the summer after my freshman year of college. Having had a license but no car for several years, I had built up some serious "need for speed" angst, and all that anticipation came gushing out like gasoline to fuel my new passion. I probably drove four thousand miles that first summer. The MR2 and I were inseparable. I drove my little five-speed with the pistol-grip shifter up and down sunny California, back and forth from friends' houses, concerts, camping trips, and plenty of just-for-fun adventures.

That poor old car didn't know what to do with this young driver who wanted to fly down the freeway at breakneck speeds for hours on end. So, only a few months into our relationship, it told me what it thought of my reckless driving habits. It said the only thing it *could* say to get my attention:

## CHECK ENGINE

Those eleven orange letters caught my interest all right. But the problem was, I had no idea *what* to check. I was a nineteen-year-old who barely knew how to change the oil or fix a flat. And that four-cylinder engine was crammed into a tiny compartment at the back of the car. I was in way over my head. So I did what every logical nineteen-year-old would do: I just kept driving, hoping to high heaven that light would make itself go away.

The next sign of trouble was the large pool of amber-colored liquid under my car every time I'd park for more than five minutes. Hmmm. Couldn't just wish *that* away. But having spent every last dime to buy the car, I didn't have the cash to take it to the shop. A kind family friend offered to take a look. His prognosis was even more depressing. He predicted I'd have to spend almost as much fixing the car as I did buying it in the first place. So rather than give up my social freedom, I bought a few cases of oil and poured in a bottle every time I needed to go somewhere. Seriously. I *did* that.

Soon I was spending more money on oil than on gas, and eventually I even needed to stop mid-trip to top off. My school parking space resembled an offshore oil spill. Something had to be done before Greenpeace started protests. The symptoms were all there, plain as day. My car was broken. I just didn't know *what* was broken.

Eventually I mustered up enough cash (and courage) to take my trusty ride to a mechanic. After conducting a diagnostic test, the nice man in the greasy jumpsuit smiled as he gave me the news: "Miss, your oil hose got disconnected." A forty-stinking-dollar hose had come loose. Are you *kidding* me?! I was too ashamed to mention that I had spent *five times* that much money on oil since buying the car. That's information he just didn't need to hear and which I'm still ashamed to admit.

The news of the easy fix brought both excitement because I could stop singlehandedly funding Exxon and discouragement because the fix had been within my reach all along.

The mechanic replaced the hose, and the symptoms stopped immediately. No more "check engine" light. No more greasy parking spaces. No more asking for cases of oil for Christmas.

In the days since my first car trouble, I honestly haven't learned much more about cars. My automotive skills still mainly consist of changing my oil and fixing a flat. But I'll tell you one thing I'm really good at now: going to a mechanic when the "check engine" light comes on!

At this point you might be wondering, *Um, Jessie? Just what does your broken car have to do with my secret sins?* A whole lot, actually.

Like the "check engine" light on my Toyota, our secret sins warn us that something is wrong under the hood of our hearts. Something is disconnected. We can either ignore the symptoms (maybe because somebody told us they'd be too "expensive" to fix) or get to the root of the problem.

When that orange light lit up on my dashboard, I was tempted to think the light itself was broken. I hoped it would just go away if I let it be. Talk about idiotic. The whole point of a "check engine" light is to *check the engine*! In the case of my car, the light was trying to tell me that my oil hose was disconnected. In the case of your heart, your secret sin (coping or craving in unhealthy ways) also indicates something isn't quite right. I believe your secret sin is trying to tell you something—namely, that your relationship with God has been disconnected.

## The Connection

Jesus understood the importance of connection. He once explained to His disciples just what—or whom—we need to be connected to in order to survive. But instead of a car, Jesus turned to a vineyard to illustrate His point:

> I am the vine; you are the branches. Those who remain in me, and I in them, will produce much

fruit. For apart from me you can do nothing.
Anyone who does not remain in me is thrown away
like a useless branch and withers. . . . When you
produce much fruit, you are my true disciples. This
brings great glory to my Father.

JOHN 15:5-6,8

I love this metaphor (perhaps because of an obsession with
farming you'll hear about later). I can picture Jesus walking
through a vineyard as He gives the illustration. He explains
that He is the strong and sturdy vine growing up from the
ground and nourishing all the smaller, thinner branches. I
imagine He may have cradled an immature cluster of grapes
in His hand as He explained that if the disciples wanted to
grow fruit in their own lives, they would have to stay connected to Him. Maybe He even tore off a small branch as
He talked, showing the disciples just how fast the branch and
leaves withered when the connection was broken. Jesus was
trying to cement in their minds one enormously important
truth: They needed Him for their spiritual survival.

We *need* Jesus.

As Christians, we can't survive without the life-giving
nourishment He provides. Anytime our connection to
Jesus—to the vine—is broken, we begin to wither. Oh, we
might be able to coast on the "reserves" stored in our hearts
for a bit, but the spiritual decline begins the minute that
connection is compromised.

Obviously, a branch can't produce grapes if it has been

chopped off the vine, but it also can't make grapes if its connection to the vine is strangled. My personal connection to Jesus has more often been choked than completely cut off. I've let all sorts of stuff squeeze my relationship with God, limiting the amount of spiritual nourishment I received. Mine was often a slow starvation. I didn't realize just how badly my connection to Jesus was suffering until I started to see my leaves wilt, and by then I was in serious trouble. I'm convinced I'm not alone. In the entertainment-driven, distraction-prone world we live in, well-meaning Christians who really do love God are starving to death left and right. I don't want you to be one of them!

## The Culprits

So what can strangle our connection to our Savior? If He is the source of life, what keeps us from getting the unhindered nourishment we need? Let's look at a few of the most common culprits.

### Sin

Like a "check engine" light, our secret sin is often a symptom that something is broken in our hearts. But continuing in sin also plays an active role in strangling our connection to Jesus. We can't "remain in" Jesus while at the same time doing the opposite of what He says, right? We can't receive the nourishment we need from Him when we cope or crave in unhealthy ways. If we want to stay connected to Jesus, we have to break ties with our sin. The old way of life has to go. The apostle Paul writes,

> I insist—and God backs me up on this—that there be no going along with the crowd, the empty-headed, mindless crowd. They've . . . let themselves go in sexual obsession, addicted to every sort of perversion.
>
> But that's no life for you. You learned Christ! . . . Since, then, we do not have the excuse of ignorance, everything—and I do mean everything—connected with that old way of life has to go. It's rotten through and through. Get rid of it! And then take on an entirely new way of life—a God-fashioned life, a life renewed from the inside and working itself into your conduct as God accurately reproduces his character in you. EPHESIANS 4:17-24 (MSG)

Wow. Well said. If we want spiritual health, we need to break the connection we have with our old, rotten, sinful life and "take on an entirely new way of life"—a life sustained by the true Vine, free from sin.

## Busyness

School, sports, drama, youth group, homework, debate club, work, Bible study group, shopping, music lessons, college applications, summer internships, texting—do you ever feel as though your life never stops? If so, you're definitely not alone. People are busy. Crazy busy. As in, never *not* busy.

Our preoccupation with doing "stuff"—even really good and meaningful stuff—takes a toll on our lives. The stress most of us girls experience on any given day is outrageous, and it's affecting our health, happiness, and relationships. The anxiety that comes along with overbusyness can even push us toward secret sins. It should come as no surprise that a hectic schedule affects our relationships with God. But you might be surprised to hear that allowing stress, worry, and busyness to crowd out our relationships with God isn't anything new. In fact, Jesus mentioned that very danger in a parable He once told about a farmer:

> The farmer plants the Word. . . . The seed cast in
> the weeds represents the ones who hear the kingdom
> news but are overwhelmed with worries about all the
> things they have to do and all the things they want
> to get. The stress strangles what they heard, and
> nothing comes of it.
>
> MARK 4:14,18-19 (MSG)

Did you catch that? Busyness—and the stress that comes with it—strangles the Word of God in your life. And that's dangerous because God's Word is a prime weapon for battling sin. No weapon, no victory.

In the world you and I live in, we're going to have to constantly be on guard against overbusyness. Mark 4:19 gives a stern warning that if we're not, nothing will come of the Word that God has planted in our hearts. So let me ask you this: When was the last time you spent some solid, uninterrupted, unrushed time with your Savior? Is that kind of one-on-one time with Him part of your daily routine? Do you have room in your life—here and there, throughout a week—to just be still and listen? Do you have space to confess your sin and grow in truth? Do you have time to notice Him and marvel at His beauty? If not, then make it. Do whatever you can to make it, even if you have to sacrifice some *good* things for the *best* thing. Quality time spent with God—connecting with God—allows you to receive the spiritual food you so desperately need.

## Media

Let's think for a minute about your media intake. By "media" I mean anything you watch (movies, TV shows, YouTube videos), see (pictures, print ads), read (magazines, social media sites, books), or hear (music). Simply put, just about anything and everything entertaining. How much do you think those media sources affect your connection to Christ?

I think most of us can admit that the messages we hear through the media run opposite of what God's Word says, but not many of us understand just how deeply those messages affect us. How about you? Have you soaked in so much secular culture that you're kind of numb to its effects? Would the music playing through your earbuds be welcome in church? Are you so used to seeing immodest pictures that you can walk right past a Victoria's Secret storefront ad—with gargantuan bare ta-tas stretched across the windows—without flinching? Do you justify ingesting an entire magazine (along with articles like "10 Ways to Drive Him Crazy in Bed") because of the great makeup tips on page 86? Have thousands of pictures of "skinny" or "hot" convinced you that you're not beautiful enough?

When you're getting an IV drip of media all day, every day, you start relying on it. You get numb to its presence but become super-aware of its absence. Not sure whether media controls you? If you have a quiet moment, do you automatically reach for your phone or turn on a song or flip on the TV? Are you okay with sensory silence?

Not all media is bad. Some can be useful; some can be uplifting; some is neutral. I'm not saying we should (or could) avoid media altogether. We just have to be careful that movies and Facebook, sitcoms and the Internet don't choke out our relationship with Jesus. Media can pull our attention away from God. If we want to stay connected to Jesus, we can't let media choke the life out of our relationship with Him.

Sometimes we don't know how greatly media has affected us until we go without it for a while. I've been forced to give it up a few times while traveling overseas. Let me tell you, after a few weeks (sometimes months) without the TV, Internet, magazines, or music telling me who I should be, what I should want, and how I should get it, my heart reconnected to God and I was a different person! It's kind of crazy, but I shouldn't be surprised. The Bible warns that a love of the world—including the world's entertainment—crowds out a love for God.

> Do not love this world nor the things it offers
> you, for when you love the world, you do not have

the love of the Father in you. For the world offers
only a craving for physical pleasure, a craving for
everything we see, and pride in our achievements
and possessions. These are not from the Father,
but are from this world. And this world is fading
away, along with everything that people crave. But
anyone who does what pleases God will live forever.

I JOHN 2:15-17

"Craving," "pleasure," "pride"—yep, that pretty much
sums up what the world offers us through the media's bull-
horn. According to John, if we love those things, we don't
truly love God. Ouch. But if we do truly love God, the
media—with all its faulty messages—should start to lose
its appeal. Facebook, the latest iTunes sensation, and this
month's edition of *Teen Vogue* are all fading away, so we might
as well cut them loose from our "branch" before they take
us with them.

If you're up for the challenge, I highly recommend a
media "fast." To fast means to go without something for a
certain amount of time for a specific purpose. Usually people
fast from food, but fasting from media can be just as spiritually profound! Sound intimidating? Start with just a week
or even only a few days. Instead of turning to your favorite
media, use your spare moments to reopen your connection
with Jesus. Spend time praying, journaling, or just being still,
listening for what messages He wants to give you instead of
what lies Satan wants you to hear.

## YOU MAKE ME FEEL LIKE ~~DANCING~~ SINNING

Music moves us. It touches something deep within our souls. That's why an epic anthem in a movie makes us want to cheer. A playlist filled with love songs sparks romance. Funky, fast beats motivate us to push through that last mile of a long run. Soft instrumentals melt away stress.

Have you ever wondered why music moves us so much? The simple answer is that God made it that way. God loves music! That's why heaven is filled with song (see Revelation 5:9; 14:3; 15:3). Our love for music was part of the package when He made us in His image.

Music has a profound ability to open our souls. In the context of the pure, God-focused worship He originally intended, that vulnerability allows Him to move our hearts in larger-than-life ways. But when sin entered the world, it also tainted our music. We stopped playing our music to express love for God and began using it to glorify things He stands against. Now when music opens our souls, it makes us vulnerable to swallowing ideas we might otherwise reject.

Think about it: If you overheard me telling a guy, "You can't have my heart and you won't use my mind, but do what you want with my body," you'd have the good sense to see I was an idiot.[1] But through the medium of a good dance beat, suddenly Lady Gaga's words aren't so repulsive. I've been totally guilty of this. Now that I have the luxury of hindsight, I can see—like a blaring spotlight—the effects my music had on me.

One particular album really affected me. I listened to it all the time. Without meaning to, I memorized every word. Subconsciously, the music made me feel alive, dangerous, and a tinge rebellious. I thought it was harmless. I didn't see the connection between listening to that music and a bigger temptation to sin until years later. I'm not saying the songs *made* me sin, but they sure set the stage. To this day when I hear a song from that album—at the grocery store, on TV, wherever—I have flashbacks of that dark, sinful time of my life. I can't stand to listen to that album anymore.

I still love good music. But now I stick to artists who point me *to* God instead of away from Him. This is my new criterion:

> Don't cope or crave in unhealthy ways; that will ruin your life. Instead, let God's Spirit fill you up till you overflow with praise to God! Sing God-honoring music, with melodies that move your heart to thank God for everything He is and does through Jesus.
>
> EPHESIANS 5:18-20 (MY PARAPHRASE)

We can't make the mistake of writing off the music we listen to as "just" entertainment because it affects us on a deeper level. If you're serious about staying connected to Jesus and about overcoming your secret sins, you need a life sound track that is going to pump you up and draw you closer to Him. A simple exchange—unholy tunes for virtuous ones—has the power to radically transform your life.

## Friends

The people you hang out with have a huge impact on you. That impact can be positive or negative and is rarely neutral. The saying "Bad company corrupts good character" isn't just a well-meaning phrase; it's Bible-backed truth! (See

1 Corinthians 15:33.) Of course, we don't always get to choose who we spend time with (we can't pick our coworkers or neighbors, for example), but when we do have a choice, it's wise to give our friend choices some thought.

The book of Proverbs has a ton to say about friendships: what kind of friends to look for, who to watch out for, and how to be a good friend. You should check it out. If your friends aren't helping you stay connected to the Vine, there's a chance they are strangling your connection to Him. That's a big deal. So how do you know which type of friends you have? Here are some questions that might help you decide:

- What is the number one topic of conversation when you're together or chatting online?
- How often do you talk about God?
- Do you ever feel pressure to do something you know isn't right?
- After you hang out with your friends, do you feel better about yourself or worse?
- Are your friends Christians? (They don't have to be Christians to be good friends, but if they *do* believe in God, they should act like it.)
- Would you say your friends have high moral standards? Do they respect and support you for yours?

Choosing to break ties with less-than-stellar friends is one of the most difficult decisions you may ever have to make. You could face your share of solo lunches and lonely Friday nights because of it. Is your connection to Jesus worth the pain? Absolutely. I can't emphasize enough that the people you hang out with will either lead you toward Jesus or pull you away from Him. Be choosy. Wait for friends who are going to *act* like friends: calling you out when you're wrong, lifting you up when you're down, and pointing you to God when you're confused. Those kinds of friends are priceless. (So make sure you're *being* that kind of friend too!)

## Guys

Ah . . . *guys*. The most delightful distractions from the true Vine—agreed? But as innocent as those handsome eyes may seem, a preoccupation with guys can hijack your relationship with Jesus faster than a lion snagging his prairie lunch. Trust me.

The apostle Paul knew that while marriage is a gift from God, relationships also affect the amount of time and intimacy we have with Him. That's why Paul laid this out there for the Corinthian women:

> I want you to be free from the concerns of this life.
> . . . A woman who is no longer married or has never
> been married can be devoted to the Lord and holy
> in body and in spirit. But a married woman has to
> think about her earthly responsibilities and how to
> please her husband. I am saying this for your benefit,
> not to place restrictions on you. I want you to do
> whatever will help you serve the Lord best, with as
> few distractions as possible.
>
> 1 CORINTHIANS 7:32,34-35

Even though Paul was talking about marriage, the principle applies to any type of romantic relationship. When you're in love with a guy—even a really good guy—you end up splitting your time, thoughts, and affections that were once God's alone.

Look, I'm married, and I'll be the first to tell you that marriage is amazing—a beautiful gift from God. But I also have to agree with Paul. We are limited creatures; we have only so much energy, emotion, and time to give. A romantic relationship (even just the pursuit of one) divides those resources. Worth it? Absolutely, *when* the relationship is in God's timing and done God's way.

But if the "check engine" light is on because you have issues "under the hood" of your heart, a relationship can keep you from dealing with them. All those butterflies, hopes, and dreams can drown out Jesus' voice. And if your secret sin is wrapped up in that relationship, you're in danger of dying off completely if you don't break the stranglehold that relationship has on your heart.

Are you obsessed with love and romance? Have you allowed a guy to take God's rightful place as the center of your world? Has sexual sin calloused your heart? If so, it's time to get reconnected to Jesus. He will satisfy your heart's deepest longings!

## The Test

We know that our secret sins are like a "check engine" light on the dashboards of our hearts, warning us of deeper issues.

But that's a pretty limited test. We can't rely on secret-sin-frequency alone to determine whether we're spiritually healthy. We have other areas of our lives that must be monitored. So how can we know whether we're thriving and growing in our relationship with God? Whether we're connected to the Vine by "remaining" in Him?

*Look at the fruit.*

Remember John 15? Jesus said that if we stay connected to Him the way we should, we'll see fruit growing under our bushy green leaves (see verse 5). Fruit grows on healthy branches. No fruit? No bueno.

Galatians 5 builds on Jesus' illustration by explaining just what that fruit should look like. It's the farm-fresh produce of the Holy Spirit, and it looks, smells, and tastes worlds different from our sin. Here's a quick look at the differences:

| Sinful Desires[2] | Fruits of the Spirit[3] |
| --- | --- |
| Sexual sin | *True* love |
| Idolatry | Faithfulness to God |
| Substance abuse | Self-control, goodness |
| Anger, rage, and anxiety | Peace, and patience with others |
| Pleasure hunting | Self-control, goodness |
| Jealousy, envy | Joy (in what God has given you and who He has made you) |
| Arguing, fighting | Kindness |
| A selfish, me-first attitude | Gentleness (caring about others) |

Well, would you look at that? I think just about every secret sin falls somewhere in the left-hand column, which means we now have a very clear diagnostic test to help us figure out whether we're properly connected to the Vine. If we want to know whether we're growing and thriving—whether we're connected to Jesus—all we have to do is look at the fruit in our lives (the right-hand column). The health of the fruit reveals the health of our connection to Jesus. And when our connection to Jesus is unhindered, our secret sins don't stand a chance.

I love how Paul wraps up his discussion about fruit:

> Those who belong to Christ Jesus have nailed the passions and desires of their sinful nature to his cross and crucified them there. Since we are living by the Spirit, let us follow the Spirit's leading in every part of our lives. GALATIANS 5:24-25

Amen? Let's walk in step with the Spirit in every single nook and cranny of our lives, from our friends and relationships to our music and schedules. When we do, the sinful "passions and desires" you and I have been battling for so long won't haunt us anymore. They'll stay nailed and crucified to the Cross.

> *God, I admit that I haven't kept You in Your rightful place in my life. I've let so many other things crowd and limit our relationship. Thank You for being a patient gardener! I want to stay connected to Jesus, drinking in spiritual life instead of slowly starving to death. So show me the areas in my life that need to change, and then give me the courage to tackle them. I want to walk in step with Your Spirit, producing good fruit in my life! Amen.*

## Discussion Questions

1. If our secret sins are like "check engine" lights, warning us that something isn't quite right spiritually speaking, what deeper issue might your sin be warning you of?

2. What questions could you ask yourself to test whether your connection to Jesus is strong or being strangled? Write them down in your journal.

3. Of the five culprits that often strangle our connection to Jesus (sin, busyness, media, friends, and guys), which do you find most dangerous? Would you add any culprits to that list?

4. Think about your favorite music. If you actually believed and acted on the words you listened to, what decisions would you make? What would your life look like?

5. *Think of three changes you could make that would help strengthen your connection to Jesus. Write them down in your journal, and then make a plan to put those changes into practice.*

6. *Look at the chart on page 61. Which sinful desire does your secret sin fit in with? What is the corresponding fruit of the Spirit to the right of that sinful desire? What is one way you could start practicing or growing in that spiritual character trait?*

## CHAPTER 4

# Calling Sin Sin and Learning to Forgive

The day started out like a scene from *The Sound of Music*. We had spent the morning in American Basin, an 11,600-foot-high alpine paradise nestled in the San Juan Mountains of Colorado. The meadow was full of midsummer wildflowers, just as we had hoped. I half expected Fräulein Maria to appear with a quick chorus of "The hills are alive . . ." as we wound along the trail. Columbine, elephant flower, Indian paintbrush, harebell—it looked like a rainbow had exploded on the valley floor, the color interrupted only by a bubbling mountain stream that meandered through the foliage. Yeah, it was pretty sweet.

But as we drove back down the windy, rocky dirt road toward camp, disaster threatened an otherwise-perfect day.

As we bumped along, we came to a narrow, single-track section of road that perched precariously over a *very* steep, *very* long drop into a canyon. And wouldn't you know, a truck was on its way up just as we were on our way down. We were at an impasse. So after conversing with the truck driver, I began to walk up the hill to let the other drivers behind us know that we'd all have to back up until we could find a turnout to let the truck pass. The first vehicle I came to was a blue SUV.

After I explained the situation to the driver, she began backing up, only she was so miffed at the truck's driver for making us reverse that she didn't notice that her wheels were turned the wrong direction. Instead of backing up the hill, she was backing off the cliff. As her tires started going over, I ran to her window.

"Ma'am, you need to get out of your car . . . *right now.*" My voice was calm but firm.

"No, I can do this," she insisted. But as she tried to back away from the edge of the sheer drop, her tires slipped even further off the dirt road. Time to panic yet? I reached through her open window with my right arm, looking for the lock to open the door to pull her out myself.

"Ma'am, *please.* You've *got* to get out of your car!" I pleaded. Now her rear driver's-side wheel was off the ground, and her front passenger side wheel was dangling over nothingness. Didn't she see that if she didn't get out of her car, she was going to die? Was she really completely blind to the imminent danger threatening her very existence?

I began praying, out loud and with conviction, "God, hold this car up! Send your angels to hold these tires up until she gets out of her car." Lucky for all of us, God loves to show up when He's all the chance we've got. I'm happy to report that He held that car up. Eventually (read: a few seconds that felt like an eternity later), I got her door open and hung on to it with all the body weight I could muster because, certainly, little ol' me would be a big help to those angels keeping two and a half tons of metal from tumbling down the cliff.

Thankfully, the driver finally abandoned the notion that she could fix this herself and frantically unbuckled her seat belt. Still holding the door with my left arm, I grabbed her arm with my right hand and pulled.

Safely outside the car, she saw just how desperate her situation had been. She literally could have died. If God hadn't graciously intervened, her blue SUV—with her inside it—would have found its home among the other mangled wrecks at the bottom of that canyon (and I found out later there were quite a few). But instead she was safe, and now three big boys from Oklahoma climbed onto her rear tire and bumper to weigh down that car until help could arrive.

Her name was Rita. We sat on the roadside for three hours together (along with the Oklahoma trio on her bumper and a growing crowd of people trapped by the roadblock) while we waited for the tow truck that would eventually lift her vehicle to safety. Because she was pretty much stuck with me, I talked with her about God. A lot. I figured God must have a pretty amazing plan for her, as He dramatically spared her life and all that, so she might as well get to know Him a bit. She didn't surrender her life to Jesus that day, but she couldn't deny God's existence any longer. I'm praying that one day I'll see Rita in heaven and get to hear the rest of the story—perhaps how that dramatic day opened her eyes to just how much God loves her and that she lived to see many more miracles in her life.

As I think about that story, I'm struck by a sobering reality: Rita didn't understand the desperateness of her situation. There she was, tipping over the side of a sheer drop-off, and she thought she could fix it herself! *How could she be that blind?* you and I might be tempted to wonder. But before we're too hard on Rita, will you consider another sobering reality with me?

*We're just like her.*

Sin blinds us—you and me—to the desperateness of our situations. It keeps us from seeing the danger we're in. Here's the deal: If you are caught in habitual sin, you are dangling on the side of a spiritual cliff. I can't in good conscience sit here and tell you that it's no big deal. I can't just pat you on the shoulder and say, "Don't worry about it, girlfriend. We all have our struggles. Just keep trying harder and you'll be okay in the end." Please hear me on this. You won't be okay in the end if you continue in your sin. And I'll have to answer to God if I don't warn you just how dangerous willful sin is.

Just as Rita was oblivious to the extent of her personal peril, we can also be blind to the danger of our sin. So if you're caught in a secret sin of any kind today, let me stand outside your car window and tell you exactly why you need to get out right now.

## Sin can have physical consequences.

In chapter 2, we discovered that one of the common denominators between most secret sins is that they are sins against our own bodies. That's true both spiritually and physically. If you keep starving yourself, your body is going to suffer. If you keep cutting, your body is going to suffer. If you keep drinking or doing drugs, your body is going to suffer. If you have sex, you increase your chances for STDs or unplanned pregnancies. You might feel invincible now, but that's the blindness talking. Some serious consequences are probably lurking just under the surface of your skin.

## Sin can have emotional consequences.

Our secret sin has pretty negative emotional consequences as well, which is ironic, as many of us are sinning to try to cope with negative emotions. The battle with sin drains us emotionally; it steals our joy and leaves us bitter and cynical. We end up spending so much emotional energy on our pain and subsequent sin, which leads to more pain, that we have next to nothing to offer anybody else. Sin makes us emotional takers instead of life-offering givers.

## Sin always has spiritual consequences.

Most important, every secret sin keeps us from the very thing we need most in this life and the next: God. And though our Father is slow to anger and full of love (see Psalm 103:8), He is also a just and holy God (see Isaiah 5:16). He has given His children the incredible gift of the Holy Spirit, who leads us into truth, frees us from the power of sin, and renews our thoughts and attitudes, just for starters.[1] But if our hearts are jammed full of unconfessed sin, the Spirit is going to get buried under it. He'll still be with us, but He won't be able to do much in our lives. We must be free of spiritual clutter if we want to hear His voice. We need to unclutter our hearts if we want His presence to have power in our lives.

## No Excuses?

I think there's another reason we can't see just how badly we're suffering from the effects of our sin. We don't see how close our own sin is getting us to the cliff because we're focused on someone else's sin.

Let me ask you this: Were you originally tempted to sin because someone else first sinned against *you*? Think about that question for a minute. What caused you to feel so desperate to numb the pain that you took a razor blade to your arm? Were your parents fighting? Had you just read a bully's message about you on Facebook? Or what first made you aware of your sexuality? Did someone force it on you? Were you abused or raped? What made you think that you needed to be thinner to be beautiful? Did a parent or some guy say hurtful things to you? Did some big company's marketing campaign—out to make money at your body image's expense—make you doubt your true beauty?

Our secret sins often became tempting at first because of someone else's sin.

And you know what? It's okay to acknowledge that fact, as long as we realize it doesn't excuse our own sin. The Bible tells us that we all have sin hiding out in our hearts. Jeremiah 17:9 pulls no punches: "The human heart is the most deceitful of all things, and desperately wicked. Who really knows how bad it is?" We sin because we're sinful humans, and we can't go blaming others for our mistakes. Yes, someone else might have first sinned against us, but we can't make the easy mistake of focusing on their sin while ignoring the danger in our own.

So what should we do with the reality that someone else really hurt us? For starters, we can allow God to use it.

Hebrews 12 has some mighty encouraging things to say about how we can allow suffering, even suffering caused by others, to act as God's discipline in our lives. But before we look at this verse, I need you to understand that in this context, *discipline* does not always mean *punishment*. God didn't send an abuser to your door because you did something wrong. This is extremely important to understand. In this passage, the Greek word translated "discipline" is *paideia*,[2] which means tutoring, education, or training. So yes, when we sin, God sometimes "trains" us with punishment, just like any loving Daddy. But that's not always the reason for discipline. *Paideia* refers to any suffering in our life that God can use to teach or train us (which includes absolutely every-thing bad in our lives).[3] So now that we understand that in this passage, discipline isn't God's punishment, let's get to the good stuff:

> God's discipline is always good for us, so that we might share in his holiness. No discipline is enjoyable while it is happening—it's painful! But afterward there will be a peaceful harvest of right living for those who are trained in this way.   HEBREWS 12:10-11

God can use others' sin to challenge, teach, and train us if we'll let Him. But that means giving up the right we think we have to focus on what those people did to us. It means we have to stop despairing or judging or resenting their sin. In a word, it means we have to *forgive*. The people who wronged us? God will deal with them on His terms (see 2 Corinthians 5:10), but how and when that happens is up to Him. We might never see justice done in this life. Can you trust that God is good, true, holy, and fair, even if people who have hurt you don't seem to get what they deserve?

We can't control whether people sin against us, but we can control our response. We can either allow God to use our pain for our good or go kicking and screaming through it. We can respond to others' sin with forgiveness, or we can respond with sin of our own. We have the power—and the responsibility—to choose.

I love the next two verses in Hebrews 12. What should the truth about God's *paideia* inspire us to do?

Take a new grip with your tired hands and strengthen
your weak knees. Mark out a straight path for your
feet so that those who are weak and lame will not fall
but become strong.   HEBREWS 12:12-13

Here's a really, really, *really* hard truth, sis: God doesn't
excuse us from living His way, even in the really tough situations of life. Even in the face of intense suffering, He expects
us to act like the Holy Spirit–empowered, royal children of
the King we are! Are you feeling weak and tired from the
suffering you've endured? Are you dizzy from the cycle of sin
you've been spinning on? If so, it's time to take a new grip
with your tired hands. It's time to get up, dust yourself off,
and do business with God.

## Dead Meat

*Hamartiology.* Sounds like what might happen to your arter-
ies after Thanksgiving dinner, right? In the world of theol-
ogy, hamartiology is the study of sin. *But if we're forgiven,*
you might wonder, *why do we need to study sin?* I'm glad
you asked.

Imagine that you're getting ready to tour Auschwitz-
Birkenau in modern-day Poland. That brick-faced building
at the end of a long railroad track might not mean much
to you. It might be kind of boring, to tell you the truth.
But imagine touring Auschwitz-Birkenau after first taking a course at school about the horrors of the Holocaust.

Then that building wouldn't be simply another tourist stop; instead, your heart would break at what you saw, knowing that millions of men, women, and children were murdered there by the Nazis during World War II.

Sometimes a little history is all it takes to bring a sobering reality to life.

That's why we need hamartiology. We need to understand the history of our sin and how it destroys us and separates us from God. We have to get a handle on all the messy consequences of our sin before a tour of freedom will move our souls to sing "Amazing Grace." We can't fully appreciate the gift God offers us until we understand the desperateness of our situation.

So, hamartiology . . .

Sin is simply anything we do that is opposite of what God has asked us to do (see 1 John 3:4). God has a righteously, ridiculously high standard, and everyone has missed it (see Romans 3:23). He expects us to "be holy because [He is] holy" (1 Peter 1:16). *Right—just be holy. No biggie, God. I'll get right on that.* Obviously, God's command to be holy is impossible to obey on our own. And the bad news for us is that the "payment" for our sin (what we deserve) is death (see Romans 6:23). I'm talking about eternal, separated-from-God, backing-off-a-cliff, mangled-SUV death. And I don't want you to be blind to the danger you're in. We're like Rita, with two wheels dangling over the cliff, and if God hadn't intervened on our behalf, we'd all—each and every one of us—be destined to hit the bottom and shatter.

But God did intervene. Praise God, He did intervene! Jesus Christ made a way for us to escape the death we deserve. And here's the best part: He offers it to us for free (see 6:23). We don't have to jump through hoops, do penances, or get our acts together before we can receive God's grace. Grace is, after all, getting something really good when we deserved something really bad. You can't earn something like that.

Romans 5:8-10 sums it up beautifully:

> God showed his great love for us by sending Christ to die for us while we were still sinners. And since we have been made right in God's sight by the blood of Christ, he will certainly save us from God's condemnation. For since our friendship with God was restored by the death of his Son while we were still his enemies, we will certainly be saved through the life of his Son.

## Turning Around

Because of Jesus' death and resurrection, the payment for our sin has been made. God offers us forgiveness for free, but it doesn't come automatically. This isn't like a direct deposit you set up with your bank. God expects something from us before His forgiveness takes place. Acts 3:19-20 says, "*Repent* of your sins and turn to God, *so that* your sins may be wiped away. *Then* times of refreshment will come from the presence of the Lord" (emphasis added).

Notice the order there? If you want to be restored and refreshed by the presence of the Lord—His presence that was banished by our sin—first your sins have to be wiped away. And your sins are wiped away after you repent and turn to God. Turning to God is at the heart of repentance. When you repent, you stop running away from God and start running to Him instead. You do a 180, a U-turn, a complete direction reversal.

We've talked about turning to God before, haven't we? Way back in chapter 1, we discovered that turning to God was the antidote to shame: "Those who look to him [Hebrew: *nabat*] for help will be radiant with joy; no shadow of shame will darken their faces" (Psalm 34:5). Remember how we said that looking to God meant more than just gazing up at the sky hoping for a miracle? Instead it means that we show regard for, pay attention to, and consider Him in all our ways. Similarly, just mumbling a halfhearted "I'm sorry, God" isn't true repentance. We have to repent and look to God. We've got to say we're sorry, yes, but we also have to start showing regard for God by seeking holiness, paying attention to Him by listening to His voice, and considering His heart before we break His laws.

Isaiah 55:7 says,

> Let the wicked change their ways
>     and banish the very thought of doing wrong.
> Let them turn to the Lord that he may have mercy
>     on them.
>     Yes, turn to our God, for he will forgive generously.

Changing our ways is a necessary step in turning to God, even if we've been a Christian as long as we can remember. And when we turn to God, His mercy flows wide and His forgiveness overflows generously.

Now, back to hamartiology. Understanding our sin doesn't only lead us to deeper faith in Christ; it should also help magnify just how sweet God's grace is.

## Refreshing

The best news for humans since Adam and Eve first took bites out of that forbidden fruit is that God forgives sin. Hands down, this simple truth is at the heart of the gospel (which literally means "good news." And boy is it!).

When Rita accepted that she was in danger, she went from being annoyed (at having to back up her SUV) to being afraid. And when she finally got smart, unbuckled her seat belt, practically tumbled out of her car, and saw exactly how precarious her situation had been, her fear morphed into euphoria. Standing on solid ground again, she was almost giddy, shaky with thankfulness that her life had been spared. "Saved Rita" was a different woman than the person I first talked to.

Grace does that. When we understand just how much danger we're in because of our sin, God's forgiveness moves us to elation. It makes us want to shout, "I'm alive? Seriously? Ahhh-ha-ha! Woo-hoo!" while we twirl around with our hands up in the air. (Well, that's how I respond anyway. But then, no one has ever accused me of being too reserved with my emotions!)

The gospel is good news, my friend—very, very good news for those of us trapped in sin. As we read in Acts 3:19, God wipes away our sins when we repent. But there's even more good news. Let's take another look at verse 20: "Times of refreshment will come from the presence of the Lord."

Have you ever been thirsty? I mean *really* thirsty? I have—in fact, just last week.

I was never much into plants or gardening or anything like that growing up, but for some reason, the older I get, the more I have this weird desire to be a farmer. (After conferring with friends, I've found I'm not alone in my strange fixation with dirt, seeds, and making things grow. There is, in fact, a whole subculture of normal women who just happen to turn into closet *Little House on the Prairie* wannabes in their twenties. Who knew?) So, given my new affinity for all things rural, imagine my excitement when I got a flyer at a local farmer's market that read, "Be a Farmer for a Day." *Yes, please!* So off I went, my two daughters in tow, to a farm on the outskirts of town.

The fall day started out pleasantly cool, but by the time we arrived midmorning, the temps were rising. And by the time we got into the fields at noon, we were already starting to sweat. With three hours of picking and only one water bottle between the three of us, I should have added two and two before we boarded that flatbed-trailer-turned-shuttle, which took us on a three-hour veggie tour. Yeah, we ran out of water right about at the cabbage field.

The rich smell of the soil was invigorating, but breathing in all that dust while we picked potatoes, carrots, and squash in the hot sun hardly helped our dry mouths. A smart person would have called it quits and gone back to the car, but not me. I was intoxicated with the open fields and scratching my primal itch, remember? And I may have been just plain greedy to go home with as much free food as possible. So, fifteen grocery bags of vegetables later (no joke), our tongues were sticking to the roofs of our mouths like we'd eaten peanut butter on bananas with a side of caramel. Hot, dirty, and incredibly parched, we stammered back to the farmhouse. We had one thing on our minds: water.

I've never been one to pay money for things I can get for free, but I think I shelled out three bucks to Farmer Dale for some ice-cold bottled liquid. Having been on the verge of heatstroke, water never tasted so good! We were refreshed as we literally guzzled three bottles of water, feeling the icy sting from our throats all the way down to our stomachs. *Ahhhhh*.

That's what I think of when I read about "times of refreshment" in Acts 3:20. It's as if God is saying, "When you repent and turn to Me, I'm ready to hand you an ice-cold spiritual drink to refresh your parched, weary, sin-stricken soul."

But practically speaking, what does God's kind of refreshment look like? For the answer to that, let's head back to Psalm 34 (see pages 11–13). As you read it this time, keep an eye out for all the benefits of repentance and being right with God.

What did you find? How does God refresh His daughters when we turn away from our sin and turn toward Him instead? Here's what I found. God refreshes His daughters with:

- Freedom from fear (verse 4)
- Radiant joy (verse 5)
- Shame-free living (verse 5)
- Answered prayers (verse 6)
- Protection—by way of angels! (verses 7,19-20)
- Everything we need (verses 9-10)
- A direct line to God when we call to Him for help (verses 15,17)
- His comfort when our hearts are broken (verse 18)
- Redemption (saving us from sin and evil) (verse 22)
- A safe place of refuge (verse 22)

Did you find any others?

I'm afraid the downside of ink on paper is that sometimes we gloss over some very powerful truths. I hope that list doesn't seem dry or impractical. Let's think about this for a minute. Let's really try to grasp just how refreshing those benefits of repentance are. For a soul parched by sin, freedom from fear (such as fears of failure, loneliness, rejection, and loss of control) is like a bottle of water after farming in the sun for hours. To a life on the verge of spiritual heatstroke, just knowing that God is there, that He cares, and that He promises to be close to us when we're at our lowest is like a lemonade stand in the Sahara. To a girl who can't stand to look at herself for shame over what she's done (again), God's promise of radiant joy is like jumping into a pool after hiking all day. God's promises are real. His refreshing is real.

Do you need that kind of refreshing today? Does your dry, raisin-esque heart crave *Living* Water? If it does, you're in luck. Jesus said that the water He gives keeps us from ever thirsting again, and it "will become in [us] a spring of water welling up to eternal life" (John 4:13-14, NIV).

But to reap the benefits of that water, you're first going to have to call sin *sin*, repent, and turn to God. When you do, God says,

> I will sprinkle clean water on you, and you will be clean. Your filth will be washed away, and you will no longer worship idols. And I will give you a new heart, and I will put a new spirit in you. I will take out your stony, stubborn heart and give you a tender, responsive heart. And I will put my Spirit in you so that you will follow my decrees and be careful to obey my regulations. EZEKIEL 36:25-27

All in favor of a new heart say amen! How many of us need to let Him replace a rock-hard, stubborn old heart, dried out by too much sin, with a tender, responsive, obedient and *refreshed* heart, soaked in God's Living Water? And how many of us need to start living like we understand the insane truth that God's Spirit lives inside us? He's there to help us follow God's ways—His best plan for our lives—part of which means kicking our secret sins to the curb.

As if it couldn't get any better, there's one more benefit of repentance, and I have to tell you, I've saved the best for last. In fact, I get so excited about this next aspect of God's refreshing that I've dedicated an entire chapter to help us drink it all in. It's coming up next. I can't wait!

> *Father, Daddy, I've spent too long ignoring the truth about my sin, too long thinking I can fix it on my own. But now I see that my sin is serious and I'm in danger of hurting myself big-time. Give me the courage to forgive the people who first made my sin so tempting. I accept responsibility for my own sin, and I ask You for forgiveness, God. Will You please forgive me? I'm ready to turn to You, instead of to my sin, for a way out of this pain. And I'm ready for Your refreshing! Let it fall on me like Living Water, giving new life to my soul. Amen.*

## Discussion Questions

1. *What is sin?*

2. *How is sin physically, emotionally, and spiritually dangerous?*

3. *How has God made a way for us to escape the spiritual consequences of our sin?*

4. *Has your own sin ever blinded you to just how much danger you were in?*

5. *Was the sin you're trapped in today first tempting because of someone else's sin? If so, why is it important to forgive that person (or those people)?*

6. *What does it mean to repent from our sins, and why is it so important we do so?*

7. *According to Psalm 34, what types of refreshing does God give us when we repent from our sins? Which of those promises means the most to you? Why?*

## CHAPTER 5

# Let Freedom Ring

The day was June 19, 1865.[1]

The Civil War had officially ended two months earlier, when General Lee surrendered to the North at Appomattox. But without TV, phones, or the Internet, news of the war's end traveled slower than molasses. Because Texas was the westernmost Confederate state, it got news last of all. The Union finally had to send two thousand troops to the Lone Star State, led by Major General Gordon Granger, to announce some rather important news.

The general's first order of business? Tell everyone in Galveston, Texas, "Hey y'all, the war's over—oh, and you guys lost." Then, in the hot, humid weather typical for the

Gulf of Mexico, General Granger prepared to read the next order of business: "General Orders, No. 3."

> The people of Texas are informed that, in accordance with a proclamation from the Executive of the United States, all slaves are free. This involves an absolute equality of personal rights and rights of property between former masters and slaves, and the connection heretofore existing between them becomes that between employer and hired labor.[2]

In other words, your slaves are free, and if you want them to work for you, you're going to have to pay them. Two hundred and fifty *thousand* slaves in Texas—men, women, and children who had spent their lives in bondage—suddenly heard that they were free. Can you imagine the shock? The bewilderment? The giddy whoops and hollers? Can you picture the pain-weathered faces of a dad, daughter, grandpa, or cousin as news of their freedom swept over them?

It's hard to imagine that anything could have spoiled the exciting news, but General Granger's announcement was indeed bittersweet. A grim truth was hidden between the lines of "General Orders, No. 3." Those slaves soon found out that President Lincoln had declared them free two and a half years earlier.

When Abraham Lincoln signed the Emancipation Proclamation on January 1, 1863, he abolished slavery. But of course that news hadn't traveled to Confederate-controlled states such as Texas. So men, women, and children just kept right on serving their illegal masters—picking cotton, cleaning house, chopping wood, and caring for their masters' families—because they didn't know the truth about their independence. Lincoln's declaration of freedom had no power over those who didn't know they had been freed. They just went right on being slaves.

Can you imagine finding out that you had just spent two and a half years of your life serving a—perhaps very cruel—master when you didn't even have to? When it wasn't even legal? Man. I have to admit I'd probably be fighting some resentment. I'd probably be wondering, *Why didn't anyone come tell us? How could no one feel this was important enough to cross enemy lines to let us know?*

Well, there's something I need you to know, something important enough for me to cross enemy lines to tell you.

If you're a silent sufferer and you've given your life to God, the grim truth is that you're slaving away for an illegal master. The King declared you free when Jesus took your sin and nailed it with Him to a cross. In Romans 6, Paul sounds a bit like General Granger, proclaiming freedom to those who have no idea they're already free. His message goes something like this (I highly recommend you check out the whole chapter for yourself):

> Haven't you heard? You are no longer slaves to sin!
> When Christ died, you were set free from sin's power.
> . . . He died to break the power of sin, and now He
> lives for God's glory. Now it's your turn! . . . Live like

you're dead to sin's power but alive to God through
Christ Jesus. Sin is no longer your master!
ROMANS 6:6-7,10-11,14 (MY PARAPHRASE)

Have you been serving the wrong master? Have you spent
too much time doing backbreaking labor trying to fix yourself but just keep sinking deeper into sin? I can't tell you how
happy I am to remind you of what God has already said: Your
debt is paid. You are free!

## Set Free—Now Stay Free

Paul makes it pretty clear: "Sin is no longer your master"
(verse 14). But just like the slaves who went right on serving
their illegal masters long after they had been declared free,
it's possible for Christians to be free yet keep on serving the
wrong master. Those of us who struggle with secret sins keep
right on working for a spiritual taskmaster. And that master
is cruel. Sin beats us down and tells us we're no good. It tells
us to work harder—to try to earn God's forgiveness. It tells
us that we have no choice but to sin. It tells us we're beyond
saving. Sin is an oppressive master, and it would love for us to
forget the truth of what God has already done for us—for *you*.

When you gave your life to God, trusting that Jesus paid
your way, He declared you free! God broke the chains of your
bondage and welcomed you into His family. You're not a slave
anymore; you're a daughter instead (see John 8:34-36). You
heard that right—not a slave, a daughter. Maybe you know

that and still choose to lock those shackles of sin around your ankles. And the difficult truth is, when we do that—when we go back to our sin—we have no one to blame but ourselves.

God declares us free, but we have a responsibility to *stay* free. In his "emancipation speech," Paul goes on to say,

> Don't you get it? You become a slave to whatever you choose to obey. You can keep right on sinning, which leads to death, or you can choose to obey God, which leads to a rich, righteous life. . . . You remember, don't you, that when you used to just do whatever you wanted to—whatever "felt good"— you slipped deeper and deeper into sin? It only made you more miserable! So turn to God and serve a new Master. Be a slave to right living so that you will become holy.
>
> ROMANS 6:16,19 (MY PARAPHRASE)

Because Christ died for you, you are free to choose your master. So choose wisely!

## The Power of Choice

So we're free from the power of sin, but what does that mean practically speaking? It doesn't mean that we're never *tempted* to sin. Obviously. And judging by our experience, it also doesn't mean that we *won't* sin sometimes. Obviously. Even the apostle Paul got frustrated with himself because even though God was his master, he still struggled with sin that he didn't want to commit. In fact, just after his spiritual "emancipation proclamation" in Romans 6, he lays it all out there in the next chapter, admitting:

> I have discovered this principle of life—that when
> I want to do what is right, I inevitably do what
> is wrong. I love God's law with all my heart. But
> there is another power within me that is at war
> with my mind. ROMANS 7:21-23

Paul got the struggle. He knew that "on paper" he was a free man, but in real life he still *chose* sin sometimes, even when he knew it was wrong—even when he didn't want to do it. In fact, he went so far as to say that his choices still made him a slave to sin sometimes (see verse 23). Paul, a champion of proclaiming God's freedom, struggled to remain free!

If we still sin, what does it mean to be free from sin's power—to have God as our master? It means that we don't *have to* sin. We have the choice not to. When the Texas slaves found out they were granted freedom, they had the choice to stay with their masters or go out and start a new life (and incredibly, some of them chose to stay). We, too, have that decision to make. We can continue to serve sin as our master, or we can go out and begin a new, free life.

The power of choice is at the heart of your freedom.

Not only do you have the ability to choose whether or not to serve sin, you also have the Holy Spirit inside you to help you stand against temptation. That is a serious weapon— a weapon we forget about way too often. Your secret sins might be really, really, *really* tempting, but God says they are beatable as long as He is your master. Do you remember this verse?

> The temptations in your life are no different from what others experience. And God is faithful. He will not allow the temptation to be more than you can stand. When you are tempted, he will show you a way out so that you can endure.
>
> I CORINTHIANS 10:13

You always have the choice not to sin; there is always a way out. You can resist even the most shameful, addicting, or persistent secret sin because you can do all things through Christ (see Philippians 4:13). You *can* overcome your sin— even an addiction—because you have the choice not to sin. And God's Spirit in you is greater than any temptation the world can throw at you (see 1 John 4:4). (If that sounds daunting, hang with me. I'm going to walk you through the "how to" in the next chapter.)

## Profile of the Free

Psalm 107 speaks deeply to my heart because it is a joyful song shouted out by those who have been freed. Take your time as you read through each line, thinking about how it might apply to your own life.

> Oh, thank GOD—he's so good!
>     His love never runs out.

All of you set free by GOD, tell the world!
Tell how he freed you from oppression. . . .

Some of you were locked in a dark cell,
cruelly confined behind bars,
Punished for defying God's Word,
for turning your back on the High God's counsel—
A hard sentence, and your hearts so heavy,
and not a soul in sight to help.
Then you called out to GOD in your desperate condition;
he got you out in the nick of time.
He led you out of your dark, dark cell,
broke open the jail and led you out.
So thank GOD for his marvelous love,
for his miracle mercy to the children he loves;
He shattered the heavy jailhouse doors,
he snapped the prison bars like matchsticks!

PSALM 107:1-2,10-16 (MSG)

That's me! I'm one who has been set free from the oppression of a secret sin because of God's never-ending love. I'm one who was locked in a dark cell of sin and shame because I didn't heed God's counsel—because I didn't do what His Word told me to do. I'm one who felt isolated, as though there was nobody to help me stop drowning in my pain. I'm one who finally called out to God, desperate for Him to free me from the sin I didn't want to do. And—thank God!—I'm one who watched as my Mighty God grabbed hold of that jailhouse door and ripped it off its hinges, leading me into the fresh air of freedom.

I'm here to tell the world how God freed me from oppression (see verse 2), but I'm also here to tell you that God has already done the same for you. The truth is, Jesus "shattered the heavy jailhouse doors" when He smashed them against the Cross. When Jesus conquered sin and death by dying and rising from the dead, He "snapped the prison bars like matchsticks!" He proclaimed you free on the first Easter morning, more than two thousand years ago.

So let me ask you something: Are you still sitting in your jail cell?

We've each been given the precious gift of freedom through Christ. But we have to *choose* to live as though we're free. Too many of us are just hanging out in our dark, musty, miserable dungeon of sin, waving to Jesus outside. "Thanks, Jesus, for getting rid of that door. But I'm cool in here. It's kind of cozy, actually. Hey, at least I know I can come out whenever I want now, so thanks again." It's crazy, right? But that's what we do when we stay cooped up in sin when we have been declared free.

Living like we're the free girls we are isn't always easy. I get that. In fact, when we've known only the bondage of sin for what seems like forever, we might not even know where to start. So in the next chapter, we're going to talk about some practical ways to not only *choose* freedom but also *stay* free.

*Jesus, thank You for purchasing my freedom with Your blood. I can't even comprehend just how gracious and merciful You are to do that for me, a sinner! I don't want to take the gift of freedom for granted. I don't want to stay in my prison cell any longer. I want to live as if I'm free from sin—because I am! Show me how, God. Show me how to resist temptation and choose the right Master. Help me live in light of my freedom. Amen.*

## Discussion Questions

1. *If you were one of the slaves in 1860s Texas who just found out you had been free for two years without knowing it, how do you think you would feel? What would you do as your first act of freedom?*

2. *How is sin an "oppressive master"?*

3. *According to Romans 6, we are set free from sin's power. What does that mean?*

4. Until now, have you been living like you're free, or are you still serving an "illegal master" (sin)?

5. How might your life look different if you began living like the free girl you already are?

## LEXI'S STORY

I was thirteen the first time I intentionally hurt myself. Low self-esteem, depression, and anxiety have been a part of my life for as long as I can remember. When I cut my arm, it was as if all the pain I had kept inside over the years came bursting out. As soon as I made that first cut, I remember feeling like I finally had some control in my life. Regrettably, that feeling of control was more important to me than the injuries I was inflicting on myself. I found as I continued to hurt myself that the desire for pain got greater, the injuries got worse, and my self-hatred increased.

I felt alone. I was the girl who sat in the locker room by herself during lunch. (Although none of my current friends believe me, it's true!) I didn't feel there was anybody I could trust with my secret burden, so it continued to grow heavier and heavier. I started searching online for information on depression and cutting. I can't tell you how many quizzes I filled out simply to reassure myself that I wasn't imagining my symptoms. I learned I wasn't alone and just how common cutting is, but that still didn't push me to share my secret. Why? Because I was too ashamed and afraid of others' reactions.

I've tried pretty much every "self-help" suggestion out there to try to quit cutting. Sadly, a lot of the recommendations tend to just be more mild forms of self-harm. Replacing sin with a different type of sin doesn't heal anything. But I have found a few things that do help. I learned to keep myself busy and found a good friend to confide in. I've also relied on listening to music as loud as I can while simultaneously crying and praying. I have relapsed many times, but those times are much less frequent now. Calling my sin by name and facing it head-on took away my ability to ignore or justify it. I still struggle with the temptation, but I'm happy to say I've been clean for four months now.

If you struggle with cutting, please reach out and talk to someone. I wish I had found someone who understood and could have helped me back when it all began. Be wise with whom you choose to share your struggle, though. Parents or trusted adults (school counselors, youth leaders, a pastor) would be great resources. I know it's so much easier to talk to your friends, but they really won't have the knowledge or experience to get you the help you need. If it's too intimidating to approach that trusted adult alone, ask a friend to go with you. Sometimes just having that friend there gives you the courage you need to talk about this very sensitive subject.

And if you don't struggle with self-injury, please keep an open mind if someone shares her story with you. I know it may seem impossible to understand how she could "want" to hurt herself, but if she's chosen to reach out to you, it's a huge step for her. Pray for her and for the wisdom to deal with the situation in a loving, responsible way. Please know that it's okay to go to a trusted adult with the information (despite your friend's plea for secrecy). In all honesty, your friend might feel betrayed; I know I did. However, that "betrayal" made me realize how much my friend cared. She was willing to put our friendship aside in order to get me the help that I couldn't get for myself.

I believe that God will grant me the strength to continue staying clean, and I think my journey with depression and anxiety will open the door to connect with other people who have similar struggles. I relate a lot to Paul's "thorn in [the] flesh" he talks about in 2 Corinthians: "Three times I pleaded with the Lord to take it away from me. But he said to me, 'My grace is sufficient for you, for my power is made perfect in weakness'" (12:8-9, NIV). Personally, I've asked God more than three times to remove this burden from me, and although He hasn't in the way I want Him to, He has never left my side. He has already covered me in His grace and will show His power through my weaknesses, including these painful ones.

This journey has taken me the farthest away from God, but it has also brought me the closest to Him that I've ever been. It was at my rock bottom that He made Himself known to me in ways I never could have imagined, such as visible answers to prayer and healing relationships I thought couldn't be healed. He's comforted me in my darkest hour and rejoiced with me through every victory. I wouldn't trade that for anything.

## CHAPTER 6

# Kicking the Habit

I threw my duffel bag in a corner of the hotel room, kicked off my shoes, got out a notebook and a pen, and plopped down on the freshly made bed. No time to turn on the TV, check out the beach down the road, or even take a dip in the hotel pool. Not this time. Tonight I was at the local Marriott to do deal with my sin. I had just finished reading a book that unearthed a bunch of crusty gunk in my heart (having to do with my secret sin), and I knew I needed time and space to get to the root of it all—to clean it out and start fresh.

I was sick of my jail cell, and I was ready to pray all night for freedom if that's what it took.

I sat alone, holed up in room 404 on a Friday night,

desperate to meet God in a mighty way. I was there on a mission: I wanted freedom and healing from my past and present sin. I really had no idea if or how God would do that, so my game plan was simple: I'd just keep on writing prayers late into the night, hoping God might eventually get sick of hearing me blah, blah, blah and decide to show up just to shut me up (like the persistent widow in Luke 18:1-8). So I wrote. And I wrote some more. I confessed my sin. Every. Ugly. Sin. I started with my first introduction to masturbation and moved on to every guy in my life with whom I'd committed physical sin. I asked God for forgiveness. I begged God for strength to forgive those who sinned against me, and I tried to forgive myself for all my just-plain-stupid mistakes. Then I asked for healing in my marriage because some of those old sins still had lingering effects on me even though we had been married two years.

Eleven single-spaced, frantically scribbled, tearstained notebook pages later, I had the breakthrough I had been longing for. But I have to tell you, it wasn't dramatic like the turning point in a suspenseful Hollywood flick. There was no bright heavenly light, harpy sound track, or audible voice. No angel showed up at my door to let me know that God had heard my request and would miraculously take away my secret sin. In fact, even after hours of pouring my heart out onto those pages, kneeling in prayer, and then going back to the pages, everything looked and felt pretty much the same.

But I knew *something* had happened. Something had changed. I felt a lightness in my spirit that comes when we know we're forgiven. And I had an unmistakable hope that through the Holy Spirit's power in my life, I *could* resist the temptation to sin from now on.

That Friday night, God didn't break through space and time with a blow-your-socks-off miracle. Instead, He reminded me that Jesus had already busted the jailhouse door off my cell and I had the freedom to *choose* freedom (as we talked about in chapter 5). My own shame, unforgiveness, and sin habits were keeping me in that dark cell, not a locked prison door. He had already said yes to my freedom a very long time ago; now I just had to choose it.

And I did.

That night in the hotel room marked the end of a thirteen-year addiction to masturbation as well as an end to shame over other sexual sins from my past.

Two days later, I was faced with a familiar scenario that had often led to sin. But this time I kept my mind focused on Christ and resisted the temptation. That first victory was proof that God *did* answer my prayer. He had led me gently over to the light to show me the gaping hole in the wall where my prison door had once been. He opened my eyes to see that freedom had been mine for the taking the minute I had given my life to Him many years before. That day marked the start of breaking the addiction, and in His grace, I have never gone back to those deadly chains.

I wish I could tell you that after my night of prayer and fasting Marriott-style, I never dealt with sexual temptation again. But I *was* tempted. I wish I could tell you that shame over my past has never resurfaced. But it *has* taunted me. I wish I could tell you that I've never had to *re*-forgive certain people from my past who wounded me so, so deeply. But I *have* had to forgive, "seventy times seven" (Matthew 18:22). I wish I could tell you those things, but then again, maybe I don't. Our struggle against sin will *always* be a reality this side of heaven. I don't want to give you the false hope that freedom from sin (in the larger, spiritual sense) means you'll never be tempted to sin. You probably will be. Even Jesus was tempted (see Hebrews 4:15). But He chose not to sin, and we have that same choice because of His death and resurrection.

There's an old saying, "God doesn't keep the birds of temptation from flying over our heads. He only asks that we keep them from building nests in our hair." That's what this chapter is about—about keeping temptations from setting up house and becoming habitual sin again. It's about breaking the physical addiction that often comes with a secret sin.

## The Problem of Addiction

That night in my hotel room, I was ready to roll heads on my sin. I was suited up in my spiritual armor, Ephesians 6–style, ready for the fight against the powers of darkness. I could taste victory. But humans are spirit *and* flesh, and I needed more than spiritual tactics to fight temptation when I went home and faced familiar scenarios and temptations. Most secret sins are more than just a spiritual battle. They *are* spiritual—don't get me wrong! But often there's also a physical addiction that forms when you sin over and over again. That physical addiction takes discipline and determination to beat.

I'm not a scientist. And even though I've done my share of research on neurochemicals and the physical effects of dopamine (coined "the pleasure chemical") on our brains, I'm not convinced our supersmart scientists have it all figured out either. Our brains are complex. *Really* complicated. Today's brainiest minds can't completely understand or explain the intricacies of their own gray matter. Now, I believe that good science always eventually confirms what God has already said in His Word, and when it does, it can be quite helpful. But the research on dopamine and addiction isn't conclusive yet, so I'm not going to try to offer a neat little illustration that perfectly explains the physical and mental process of addiction.

What we do know—from our own experience and from God's Word—is that when we sin, we *desire* to sin again, and again, and again. You don't have to be a neuroscientist to figure that one out. And thinking back to the lineup of secret sins in chapter 2, we remember that most sin becomes a physical addiction pretty fast. You'd probably guess that substance abuse is highly addictive (thanks to your health teacher or local D.A.R.E. officer). But did you know that sexual sin, eating disorders, cutting, even lesbian relationships can be addicting too? They create a constant desire for pleasure or control—a desire that's really hard to say no to.

In fighting against our sin, we absolutely need to be suited up in our spiritual armor. But we also need a physical game plan. We're going to get to that game plan in a minute, but first check out this interesting tidbit.

## Crack or Cash?

I recently read an article in the *New York Times* about a scientist whose research challenged what we've all thought about addictions. Trust me—it's good news for you and me.

Dr. Carl Hart was no stranger to addiction. Growing up in poverty, he watched childhood friends and even relatives turn into crack addicts. People he cared about became destitute, homeless, and hopeless. The problems of addiction were near to his heart, and he wanted to find a cure. But as he researched the behaviors and the ins and outs of addiction, his findings didn't seem to match the stereotypical drug addict who can't stop once he gets a taste. And he began to wonder, *What if addicts weren't "forced" to choose the addicting substance after all?*

Dr. Hart recruited addicts through an ad in a newspaper and got to work conducting his study. Every morning, a nurse would give the blindfolded participants a pipe with a different amount of crack in it. At different points during the day, the nurse then gave the participants two options: get another hit of cocaine or receive a reward (either five dollars in cash or a five-dollar gift card). Even though the addicts knew they wouldn't get the reward until *after* the study was over, many of them still chose the reward over the drugs, especially when the offered dose was smaller. And when the nurse upped the reward to twenty dollars, *every* participant chose the reward over the drug.[1]

Interesting, isn't it? When the addict felt that the reward was better than the drug, he chose the reward. Now, I don't believe it's always as simple as x + y = z, and I'm taking this study with a grain of salt. Real life is rarely black and white. But I do know that at our core, we all want to be happy. We'll usually (though not always) choose whatever we think is going to bring us the greatest pleasure, whether we're "addicted" or not. And that's the good news I mentioned. When it comes to beating an addiction, that principle can work in our favor.

You're not a "bad Christian" for wanting pleasure (or for not wanting pain). You just have to know where you're going to find the greatest pleasure (or the least amount of pain). Ultimate pleasure isn't found in a drug, razor blade, or sexual relationship with your boyfriend. Those are cheap substitutes for the highest pleasure. That's not just fancy Christian talk. You know it's true from your own experience, don't you? Those sinful places you usually go for happiness just don't deliver. That's why I receive so many e-mails from girls admitting such thoughts as,

> "[After my sin] I feel permanently dirty."

> "[My sin] never really helps, no matter how much I'd like to think it does."

"[My sin] takes the pain away for just a little while, and then it's back within no time."

While we're being tempted, our secret sins promise they'll bring us true happiness. But we know better, don't we? In the aftermath of sin, we're always left with a mouthful of gravel: gritty shame, emptiness, and even more pain than we started with. Our sin is a cheap substitute for God's highest pleasures.

But if Dr. Hart's study is true, then we'll choose *not* to sin—not to take the crack—only if we think the alternative is a greater payoff, a greater reward.

Do you?

Your answer to that question is so important. I can give you all the practical tips in the world for breaking an addiction, but if you're still not convinced that the reward is worth it, you won't stop choosing the "drug." Sure, you might *try* to stop sinning. You might give it a real good effort. (Haven't we all?) But until God's promises of freedom, blessing, and reward sound like a recipe for your greatest happiness, all the good intentions in the world will hit the gutter. The eight tips I'm about to give you aren't going to do jack diddly squat until you're so sick of the sickness of your sin that you're motivated to do whatever it takes to change. Halfhearted desire to stop will get you nowhere but back in your sin, even more ashamed (by another failure) than you were before.

However (and this is a big, exciting "however"), once you decide that your best happiness ultimately comes from pleasing God—when that reward is real to you—you'll have the motivation you need to break the physical, lingering addiction of your sin. And let me tell you, sister, it's going to take some motivation! The good news is, with a healthy dose of hard word, breaking an addiction is doable. That's where these tips come in.

## Eight Tips for Breaking an Addiction

There's lots of advice out there from well-meaning people who want to help you stop doing what you don't want to do. Some of it is good, and some of it really isn't all that helpful. I've handpicked each of the eight tips I'm about to share because I can vouch for the fact that they work. Are there other methods that work? Sure. But these are the most effective I've found that not only deal with the real issues but also hold true to God's Word.

### TIP #1—GET ACCOUNTABLE

If you're serious about breaking an addiction, this is the first step you need to take. In fact, of all the ways girls have shared with me that they've found freedom from their secret sin, this tip tops the charts. Hands down, finding someone to keep you accountable is the most effective tactic to keep you from sinning. When you know you'll have to fess up to someone you care about, look up to, or admire, that sin starts looking a whole lot less tempting. It goes back to the reward, right? The temporary pleasure of your secret sin looks like stale french fries compared to the reward of *not* disappointing someone who is going to ask you about your progress.

Proverbs 28:13 says, "People who conceal their sins will not prosper, but if they confess and turn from them, they will receive mercy." This verse promises two more rewards for coming clean about your sin to someone you trust: flourishing and receiving mercy. If you've done time in a prison of shame, thriving and mercy might be two rewards that make the risk of vulnerability worth it.

So, who should you talk to? In her testimony on pages 96–98, Lexi was right when she said that even though it's usually easier to talk to your friends about a struggle, the best place to find help is a trusted adult. Your mom or dad, a pastor, counselor, small-group leader, teacher—any of these could be good choices. You're looking for someone you can trust to ask you the hard questions, celebrate with you in your victories, and point you to God's grace in your failures.

You need to find someone who will ask you how you're doing in your fight against sin even before you bring it up. However, that doesn't mean you're excused from volunteering information! If you want to get the most out of your accountability relationship, don't wait to be asked how you're doing (at least not all of the time). If this person is around you a lot, they might not want to ask, "Soooo? Have you _____?" every time they see you. Maybe to avoid the who-should-bring-it-up dilemma you could schedule a set time each week or month to formally talk about your progress.

Although accountability is important as a first step, some of us need even more help in our fight against sin. If you think you might need more help, hang tight. In chapter 8, I'm going to share some places to find it.

## TIP #2—GET IN THE WORD

God's Word is a sleeper. No, I don't mean you'll fall asleep reading it. Quite the opposite. Like a sleeper agent, the Bible delivers serious success when no one sees it coming. It's the unassuming superstar that surprises everyone. It's the David that comes out of nowhere to slay our Goliath sins. God's Word has power! So if the thought of reading your Bible to break your addiction sounds like putting a bandage on a greased watermelon, I dare you to give it a chance.

God's Word "is alive and powerful" (Hebrews 4:12) and "is useful for teaching, rebuking, correcting and training in righteousness, so that the servant of God may be thoroughly equipped for every good work" (2 Timothy 3:16-17, NIV). In other words, the Bible takes your sin to the woodshed because it changes *you*. That's what Alyssa found. Here's what she says about the Bible's impact on her fight against an eating disorder:

> All of the ways that I have tried to overcome my secret sin have failed. Surprise, surprise, right? I have tried to just push the thoughts away. I have tried

journaling them. I have tried keeping a food diary.
But ultimately, those failed. They worked for a while,
yet they have all failed. What *has* worked is when I
spend time in the Word really understanding what
God says about me, about my identity, and about
my worth.

The more you get into God's Word, the more it's going
to transform you, from the inside out. Jesus said that if you
are faithful to His teaching (found in the Bible), then "you
will know the truth, and the truth will set you free" (John
8:31-32). Read the Bible, know truth. Know truth, find freedom, including freedom from addiction. As Alyssa found,
truth helps you get to the root of your sin. It changes the way
you think, empowering you to change.

The Bible is a big book, and if you're not familiar with
it, finding your way through its pages can be a bit intimidating. If you need a place to start, I suggest the book of
John. Proverbs is another great place to begin (with thirty-
one chapters, you can read one for each day of the month).
Or you could read our theme passage, Psalm 34, every day
until you memorize it. *Where* you start isn't as important as
*getting started*, so take a deep breath and dive in!

### TIP #3—CHANGE YOUR MIND

Speaking of changing the way you think, this tip is essential—
not only for finding initial freedom from an addiction but
also for staying free. Lamentations might seem a strange

book to go to for advice, but stick with me. The prophet Jeremiah said,

> Remember my affliction and my homelessness,
> the wormwood and the poison.
> I continually *remember them*
> *and have become depressed.*
> *Yet I call this to mind,*
> *and therefore I have hope*:

> Because of the LORD's faithful love
> we do not perish,
> for His mercies never end.
> They are new every morning;
> great is Your faithfulness!
> I say: The LORD is my portion,
> therefore I will put my hope in Him.

LAMENTATIONS 3:19-24 (HCSB, EMPHASIS ADDED)

Notice the path Jeremiah's thoughts took. When he focused his thoughts on his suffering, he got depressed. But when he called to mind just how kind God had been to him—how loving and faithful—he felt hope. Even though he had started out feeling really down, he changed his self-talk, and when he did, what came out of his mouth wasn't a pity party but praise instead.

Your mind is a crazy-powerful thing.

If you want to break an addiction, memorize and then live out Philippians 4:8: "Fix your thoughts on what is true, and honorable, and right, and pure, and lovely, and admirable. Think about things that are excellent and worthy of praise."

Did you know that your emotions come from the thoughts you think? So if your addiction gains traction from faulty ideas about yourself or about others (yeah, that's pretty much all of us), then you need to change the way you think if you want victory. Romans 12:2 instructs us, "Don't copy the behavior and customs of this world [where secret sins run wide and deep], but let God transform you into a new person by changing the way you think."

Changing your mind changes *you*.

Sulking isn't going to help you. Focusing on how you're a victim isn't going to help you. Rehearsing your sin isn't going to help you. What is going to help? Redirecting your thoughts to how incredibly amazing your God is! Reminding yourself daily—hourly, if necessary—that you have a choice *not* to sin. Thinking about the hope you have of freedom and how much better holiness feels than sin. Those kinds of thoughts are going to ensure your freedom.

### TIP #4—TALK TO GOD

Have you ever stopped to think about how incredible it is that God lets us talk to Him? Anytime, anywhere, any mood, any reason, we have a direct line to the great I Am. It's pretty mind-blowing to think about it, yet most of us don't take advantage of that amazing privilege nearly often enough.

Girls are the acknowledged experts on the subject of relationships, am I right? Furthermore, any girl will tell you that the key to a great relationship is communication. You can't get to know someone—let alone go deep and intimate with them—without talking. I could go on and on about how important and rich and life-changing a healthy prayer life is, but I'm going to focus on how it relates to beating an addiction (since that's what we're talking about and all). When we talk to God, whether for thirty seconds or thirty minutes, amazing things happen. We begin to see life through His eyes. We find power to overcome our temptations. We find comfort when we need His grace. So talk it up! Get to know your Lord by spending time in conversation with Him.

## TIP #5—LIVE IN THE LIGHT

Literally. Keep the lights on.

Have you ever noticed that we commit most secret sins in the dark? Think about it. When are a guy and girl most tempted to have sex? When is cutting most tempting? When do most people get drunk or high? The majority of sin happens at night, in the dark. That shouldn't be a big surprise, as the Bible makes a clear connection between darkness and sin (see 1 Thessalonians 5:7 and the passages about light on the next page). When sin has *really* hardened a girl's heart, then she starts getting more comfortable sinning in broad daylight. And trust me, that's not a good sign.

This may sound simple, but if you want to break an addiction to a sin that tempts you most in the dark, then don't be in the dark! Whenever possible, stick to the light. I realize that a girl's got to sleep at some point, but until you're tired enough to drift off into happy slumber, keep the lights nice and bright. And even when you do have to turn the lights out, have some verses about God's light memorized so you can speak them over yourself in those tempting moments.

The Bible has some great things to say about the power of light in the fight against sin and points out some really cool similarities between light and God too. I could literally write pages and pages about this, but because of space (and not wanting to bore you with my obsession with all things light), I'm going to give you some passages to look up and contemplate on your own. This would be a great time to pull out that journal we talked about in the intro. Jot down these references, read the verses, and write down anything that stands out to you. (Bonus: This will help you practice tip #2!)

Psalm 97:11
Psalm 104:2
John 1:4-9
John 3:19-21
2 Corinthians 4:6
Ephesians 5:8-14
1 Thessalonians 5:5-8
1 Peter 2:9
1 John 1:6-7

TIP #6—FIND AN OUTLET

Journal. Paint. Run. Serve. Skateboard. Dance. Sing.

Even though a hobby alone might not have the power to break an addiction, it sure can help. A healthy outlet can help you release negative emotions, force you to look outside your suffering, and give you a little fun at the same time. The type of hobby that appeals to you will depend on your personal style. Are you an artist? Athlete? Book lover? Or (likely) some combination? Try something new. You never know if you'll like it until you give it a shot! (Except competitive mooing. You probably don't need to try that one to guess your feelings about it.)

One tiny piece of advice: Don't let your fun, healthy outlet crowd out all the "space" in your life. Remember how when we get crazy busy, we can actually be more drawn to sin because of the pressures of always being on the go? Yeah, you don't want to do that. So ask God to help you find a healthy balance.

Although I love sports and the arts, I'm definitely a journal junkie. I have a box of old notebooks dating all the way back to my tenth birthday. Journaling not only lets you vent what you're feeling now, it doubles as a way to remember just how far God has brought you. If you decide to keep a journal (or if you keep one already), here's a suggestion. Instead of just venting all the negative stuff in your life (which can keep your mind focused on your suffering), make a point to move on to praise by the end. Mimic Jeremiah (see tip #3) or King David or one of the other psalmists. They knew how to pour out their aching hearts in brutal honesty, but they always came around and looked to God in their suffering before they put their pens away (see Psalm 73 for a prime example).

### TIP #7—WIN THE BATTLE BEFORE IT'S A BATTLE

Sometimes you can avoid temptation altogether with some preemptive self-discipline. Here's a "not so spiritually heavy" example of what I mean.

My oldest daughter started sucking her thumb when she was just a few weeks old. So when it came time for her to kick the habit (per her dentist's orders) five years later, it was no small task. All day long she'd be fine (thanks to a hundred-pack of her favorite gum), but as soon as we got her snuggled into bed and said good night, the temptation was just too intense. Poor thing! On one hand, she *really* wanted to stop. On the other hand (the hand with her favorite thumb), not so much. So after a few weeks of coaching her, praying for her, pleading with her, and yes, even bribing her to stop, we realized this was a battle she just couldn't fight on her own. That's when we brought in the big guns: the gloves. We took an old pair of white gloves, sewed ribbons around the wrists so we could tie them on tight, and decorated those puppies to the nines with glitter glue and turquoise beads. And guess what? (After I started quadruple-tying the ribbons so she couldn't undo them) they worked!

Win the battle before it's a battle by knowing your limits. Make it hard to sin. How can you set yourself up for success before you're even tempted? If you struggle with bulimia, don't buy foods you're tempted to binge on. If you and your boyfriend can't keep your hands off each other, don't hang out alone together, especially at night. If you struggle with cutting, don't keep sharp objects handy. You get the idea. By removing tempting triggers, you can defeat your sin before you're even tempted.

### TIP #8—FOCUS ON THE REWARD

Remember the "cash or crack" study? Rewards are powerful motivators! And it's okay to look forward to them. For Christians, breaking a sin addiction has both physical and spiritual rewards. Know the rewards. Memorize them. Write them down. Have them on the tip of your tongue so you can tell yourself why indulging in that sin isn't worth it when temptation strikes.

You can even create rewards for yourself. One girl I know went out for ice cream with her accountability partner every time she was "clean" for a certain amount of time. You've got to celebrate the victories, small and big! I have only one word of caution: Be careful not to replace an old addiction with a new one. Rewarding yourself with a cigarette when you resist a drink, or biting your lip instead of cutting, is only going to land you a new addiction. And going shopping every time you resist the urge to _____ ? That could most definitely backfire on you (and your wallet). Used wisely, though, rewards can be helpful, healthy motivators to kick a sin habit.

## The Ingredients for a Miracle

That night in the hotel room, I was unabashedly praying for a miracle. I just wanted God to take my sin—even the *temptation* to sin—and chuck it across the globe like a bad habit. But here's the deal: That's not usually the way God works. Does He help us tackle our hurts, sins, and addictions? Absolutely. But most often, He does that by simply opening our eyes to seeing that all the ingredients for a miracle were right there in front of us the whole time.

God rarely does for us what we can do for ourselves.

Salvation? God's job. Forgiving our sins? That's His department too. But taking the daily, careful steps to obey Him in every nook and cranny of our lives? Well, He usually leaves that up to us, because we *can* do it. We might not feel as if we can sometimes, but that's only because we don't understand how powerful the Spirit within us is! I mean, if the Holy Spirit can handle leading armies, empowering Sampson, transporting people cross-country, and raising Jesus from the dead,[2] I think He's got our backs in this area, too.

You might always face the temptation toward your secret sins, but those temptations grow weaker the longer you stay clean. The more you resist, the easier it becomes to resist. That's one of the beauties of breaking an addiction.

My prayer is that as you put these tips into practice, the sweet taste of God's rich rewards will blow away the gravelly taste sin leaves in your mouth. With His power in you, you *can* do this. I promise!

*Father, I want to stop sinning. You know I do. But I guess I haven't recognized the rewards of obedience or I would*

*have kicked this sin addiction already. So help me in my
unbelief, God. Help me truly see and believe that Your
rewards for a sin-free life will make me happier than my
sin. Give me courage to live as though I believe the truth.
Thank You for being so patient with my failure. I'm
ready to celebrate victory with You! Amen.*

## Discussion Questions

1. *If you've ever tried to break a sin addiction, what methods
   did you try? Did they work?*

2. *Do you have someone to keep you accountable to your sin?
   If not, whom could you ask for help in that area?*

3. *God's Word has serious power against our addictions. In
   your journal, start a list of verses that can empower and
   equip you to change. Then make a plan to read God's Word
   regularly and keep adding verses to your list.*

4. *What bogus ideas about yourself or about others have allowed sin to gain traction in your life? Write each of those thoughts down in your journal. Then, using Philippians 4:8-9 as a guide, cross out each one and replace it with a true, helpful, or encouraging thought. For example, you might replace "I'm not worth anything" with "I have worth because Jesus bought me with His blood."*

5. *Why is light a powerful weapon against secret sin?*

6. *What activities or hobbies interest you? Is there anything you've always wanted to try but haven't had the motivation to give it a shot?*

7. *How could you beat your sin before it's even a temptation? Can you think of any boundaries or safeguards you could put into practice to make it hard to sin?*

8. *Not sinning has a greater reward than the pleasure of sin, but that's hard to remember in a moment of big temptation. In your journal, list every reward you can think of— both spiritual and physical—that is yours when you choose not to sin. What rewards await you when you boot your secret sin for good? Bonus points: Write your top three on an index card and place it somewhere you'll see it when you're tempted to sin.*

## CHAPTER 7

# Mercy for a Fall

Raise your hand if you've ever been *here* before:

You're suited up in your spiritual armor, ready for war against your sin. *This time, it's for real,* you tell yourself. Bible reading, *check*. Prayer, *check*. Accountability partner, *check*. Motivational worship sound track, *check*. You even just finished reading a book about overcoming your secret sin (wink), and now you're amped to kick the habit for good. You've got the will, and you're determined to make a way. There's no way in heck you're going back to your sin.

And then—bam—*you do*.

I've been there, friend. Boy, have I been there. And in that moment—when you're heartbroken, disappointed in yourself, and maybe even a bit disillusioned—you've got two options. Just two. You can either give up or you can find a way to keep fighting.

I guess it's pretty obvious which of those two choices I think you should pick. But when you're smack-dab in the wake of regret, the choice rarely looks that simple. I mean, let's be honest—the "giving up" option has serious appeal when you're exhausted from the inner turmoil of fighting against sin and then failing again, not to mention the onslaught of mental missiles. Do any of the following thoughts sound familiar?

> *Why should I even keep trying when I know I'm just going to mess up again?*

> *How can I ask God for forgiveness when I promised Him I was going to do better this time?*

> *There must be something wrong with me.*

> *I'm never going to beat this thing.*

Yeah, they're familiar to me, too. In fact, Proverbs 26:11 is, unfortunately, a verse I am very well acquainted with: "As a dog returns to its vomit, so a fool repeats his foolishness." That verse had a way of popping into my head after every sin. Nothing like a good visual to kick you when you're down. I *knew* I was foolish to return to my vile, putrid sin, but replaying those words over and over did nothing to motivate me to change. Instead, the "I'm just like a stupid dog" mantra made me want to give up, time and time again.

If you fail, focusing on your failure is a surefire way to fail again.

So what should we do, then? When we sincerely, desperately want to stop sinning, and then slip up, how should we respond?

## Your Biggest Enemy

The prescription for repentance is the same no matter how many times you've committed a particular sin. But you do face a giant that grows bigger and bigger the longer you wrestle with your sin. This giant's name is Apathy, and he's a killer in slug's clothing.

Apathy means losing the will to fight.

I think Apathy is the single most dangerous obstacle you're going to face if your road to complete healing takes the "scenic route." We heard Apathy's voice earlier: *Why should you keep trying when you know you're just going to mess up again?* Other times he says, *This is just too exhausting. Why don't you give in—just for a little while—and then pick up the fight later?* Or *I bet no one else has tried so hard to be good, so give yourself a break!* Apathy is a master at manipulation, justification, and procrastination.

Don't be fooled by Apathy's harmless disguise. He's out for the kill. We all know the mastermind under the slug disguise, and he won't be happy until he sees you taken out of commission for the kingdom of God. Satan can't touch your salvation (see John 10:28-30), but he *can* keep tempting you to stay trapped in sin, which makes you ineffective for God's purposes. So know your enemy's tactics. Don't be taken for a fool.

## Your Greatest Ally

If Apathy is your greatest enemy when you slip up, godly sorrow is your greatest ally. The phrase *godly sorrow* comes from the second letter Paul wrote to the Corinthian church. Between you and me, those Corinthians had the corner on secret (make that not-so-secret) sins. In his first letter, Paul came down pretty hard on them. He reminded the Corinthian Christians of God's standards for purity and told them to start living like God's children instead of Hollywood hussies. (I may be paraphrasing a bit.) The letter was harsh but needed. And to their credit, the Corinthians took Paul's discipline to heart. They changed. Paul was so happy about their response that he wrote them again with these encouraging words:

> I am not sorry that I sent that severe letter to you, though I was sorry at first, for I know it was painful to you for a little while. Now I am glad I sent it, not because it hurt you, but because the pain caused you to repent and change your ways. It was the kind of sorrow God wants his people to have. . . . For the kind of sorrow God wants us to experience *leads us away from sin* and results in salvation. There's no

regret for that kind of sorrow. But worldly sorrow, which lacks repentance, results in spiritual death.

2 CORINTHIANS 7:8-10 (EMPHASIS ADDED)

Another term for "worldly sorrow" is *shame*. When we sin yet again, our natural emotion is shame. But this passage reminds us of what we discovered in chapter 1: Unhealthy shame leads to spiritual death. Godly sorrow, on the other hand, is sadness over our sin that motivates us to stop sinning.

What else does godly sorrow do in your heart? Paul continued,

See what this godly sorrow produced in you! Such earnestness, such concern to clear yourselves, such indignation, such alarm, such longing to see me, such zeal, and such a readiness to punish wrong. You showed that you have done everything necessary to make things right.

2 CORINTHIANS 7:11

Ready for a SAT-style equation? Godly sorrow is to our fight against sin as Kelly Clarkson's "Stronger" is to getting over a breakup. (Can you hear it? "What doesn't kill you makes you STRONGER . . .") Godly sorrow gets us pumped to dust ourselves off and get on living life with renewed resolve. No matter how many times we fail, we can choose to get mad at our sin. We can look our nemesis in the face and say, *"Not next time, buddy. Next time I'm not giving in, and I'm never giving up. Next time you're* mine.*"*

As you may have guessed, godly sorrow is the opposite of apathy. While apathy would have us lie down and give up, godly sorrow tells us to get up and keep fighting. It warns us to be mad about our sin, surprised by our sin, and passionate to stop our sin.

Shame has no place when you've been made radiant by looking to God. So get up when you slip up. Use your sadness over your sin to motivate you to "do everything necessary" not to do it again. Get fired up over your sin. Again and again. As many times as it takes. God's mercy *never* runs out, and neither should our quest for holiness.

## When You Slip Up

Can we agree to cross out the "giving up" option? Good. Now the only order of business is to figure out *how* to keep moving forward when we feel disappointed, discouraged, and unworthy. The key to moving forward is to understand one important truth about God: "[God's] mercies *never* end. They are new *every* morning" (Lamentations 3:22-23, HCSB, emphasis added). Why is that such a big deal? It's because between you and God, the only one who views your one hundred nineteenth sin differently than your first is *you*. God views each one the same. Every sin breaks His standard equally, and He offers the same forgiveness and mercy for every single one.

Every. Single. One.

This truth turns logic on its head. Because we're human—humans who get *tired* of others' failures—we tend to think

God is the same way. We think the more someone sins, the less they deserve forgiveness. That's how we operate, right? If your friend stabbed you in the back, you might forgive her. If she did it twice, you'd be less likely to restore your friendship. And if she did it three or four times, you'd be finding yourself a new friend! But *never-ending* mercy for a chronic backstabber? From a human standpoint, it's illogical, stupid, and weak.

Aren't you glad God defies human logic? I am! But it takes a conscious effort to replace the lies in our head (lies like "I've sinned too many times for God to forgive me") with the truth: God never runs out of mercy.

So, you're armed with a new way of thinking. Now what? What do you do when you slip up? Sorry to be anticlimactic, but it's the same thing you did (or should have done) the first time you sinned:

1. Call sin *sin*
2. Repent
3. Turn to God

It doesn't matter if it's your fourth time with a particular sin or your forty thousandth. It really is that simple—not easy, but simple. We all know those three little steps are difficult (especially the conscious effort to turn to God). But again, the hardest part is getting over the fact that God's mercy is illogical. It doesn't make sense in our little brains that God would forgive our two hundredth sin the same way He did our first. We feel as if we should have to work harder for forgiveness the further down the "sin road" we travel. And if we're really, really honest? We'd *rather* God give us some hypothetical push-ups to do to earn back His love than for Him to give us free grace for the umpteenth time. (The ugly truth hiding behind those thoughts is that we'd actually feel more comfortable earning our salvation. And boy would Satan *l-o-v-e* for you to believe that you have to earn your salvation.)[1]

## A Profile of Mercy

My college writing professor always told us, "Write what you know." It seems the apostle Paul was ahead of his time as a writer then. He wrote about the things he was familiar with, the topics he knew inside and out. And Paul knew all about godly sorrow.

You see, Paul wasn't always Super Apostle. Did you know there was a time when he *hated* the name *Jesus* and everything it stood for? Paul (known then as Saul) had heard about Jesus and decided he was a fraud. He dedicated his young life to rounding up and punishing anyone who followed that poser—that *dead* poser—who had called himself the Messiah. And as if that weren't bad enough, he conspired against and consented to *murder* a man who was full of faith, grace, and the Holy Spirit (see Acts 6:5,8; 7:58; 8:1). How's that for sin?

Paul readily admitted that because of his sin (blaspheming, arrogance, and persecuting the church, for starters), he should never have been counted as an apostle (see 1 Corinthians 15:9-10). But because of God's illogical mercy, God forgave him . . . and then chose him for a special ministry. Crazy, right? Now, knowing just how bad he had messed up, Paul could have wallowed in shame for a few decades instead of taking God up on His offer of forgiveness. But instead he allowed the godly sorrow he felt over his sin to motivate him to work "harder than any of the other apostles" (verse 10) in spreading the good news of freedom to the lost, lonely, and dying.

Maybe you've heard that story before. But have you ever wondered why God would choose to have mercy on a big screwup like Paul? That's an important question because the answer will tell us why God would have mercy on big screwups like you and like me. Paul gives us the reason in 1 Timothy 1:16: "God had mercy on me so that Christ Jesus could use me as a prime example of his great patience with even the worst sinners."

Wow! Did you catch that? God had mercy on Paul pre-cisely *because* he was a colossal sinner so that we'd know exactly how patient God is with the biggest sinners of all time. Praise the Lord and pass the freedom! You know what this means, don't you? The "worst sinners" aren't just those who commit one really big sin. I'd reckon the biggest sin-ners are the ones who have sinned more than once. Maybe even dozens (or *thousands*) of times. With the same sin. Even when they know better. *That*, my friend, would be a really big sinner. And if overcoming your secret sin has been more like a game of Chutes and Ladders than Candy Land, then congratulations—you qualify.

God has mercy on the world's biggest sinners—people like Paul and you and me—precisely because it's illogical. And God's illogical mercy in our lives is like a billboard to the masses shouting, "You think you're too far for grace? Think again. Just look at me, exhibit A!"

Paul is a perfect example of what can happen when a person accepts God's mercy and then allows godly sorrow to amp them up for a fight against sin. He went from the "worst [sinner] of them all" (1 Timothy 1:15) to a living commercial for grace. How about you? Will you let God's mercy toward your sin motivate you to work twice as hard to share the good news of freedom with others? Will you be God's next "profile of mercy"?

When you fall, embrace God's mercy. Let godly sorrow motivate you to pick yourself up, not losing an ounce of zeal against your sin. But if you find that you're slipping up on repeat, it may be time to do a little diagnostic test on your spiritual life to see if there are some bigger issues you need to work on. I'm going to show you how to do that next.

> *Father, I can't get over Your mercy. It's completely illogical! I'm so thankful that You never run out of it because, looking at my track record, You and I both know I need an unlimited supply! With everything in me, I pray that I would never do _____ again. But if, despite my best intentions, I do fail, may godly*

*sorrow motivate me to keep on fighting against sin.
I want to be a living billboard of Your mercy, pointing
others to the power of the Cross. Amen.*

# Discussion Questions

1. *Have you ever been discouraged because you seem to keep
   committing the same sin over and over again?*

2. *In your fight against your sin habit, what is your biggest
   enemy? What is your greatest ally?*

3. *When Apathy tempts you to give up, what truth can you
   throw back at him?*

4. *What is godly sorrow? According to 2 Corinthians 7:8-11,
   what can it produce in your life?*

5. *What is mercy? Why does God give it?*

6. *Do you have a hard time accepting God's mercy? If so, why do you think that is?*

## CONSTANCE'S STORY

The following story is from Constance Rhodes, author of
*Life Inside the "Thin" Cage*,[2] and founder of FINDING*balance*,
the leading Christian resource for daily help with eating
issues. I think you're going to love her as much as I do!
And if you struggle with an eating disorder (or know
someone who does), be sure to check out her website
at www.findingbalance.com.

When I was about ten years old, I began to realize that looks
were a key to getting attention and love. I was often hungry
for such things, so I began to place a lot of focus on looking
"good" so I could fill the void. As a teenager, weight wasn't
a problem for me, but I quickly gained the "Freshman 15" in
college. I was so afraid and ashamed of the weight gain that
I threw myself into desperate diets, which ultimately led me
toward more and more disordered eating patterns.

During my late teens and throughout my twenties, I was
completely obsessed with my body, my appearance, and
my weight. Every moment of every day was consumed with
thoughts about what I was eating and how much I weighed.
I was afraid of being lonely, and I wrongly believed that per-
fecting my appearance would somehow make me feel less
alone in life. Ironically, the more I became obsessed with
food and my body, the less I seemed to connect with others
in relationship, and the more isolated and lonely I felt. This
just pushed the cycle further and further.

For many years, I thought I was alone with my issues. I
knew that my mom had struggled, and I had a friend or two
in college who admitted to a similar struggle as well, but this
was before the days of the Internet and before conversations

about mental health and recovery were popular. The more I walked this journey alone, the more I justified what I was doing to myself.

I stayed trapped in my sin because somewhere inside I believed that it was actually giving me something I wanted and needed. I believed that by maintaining a particular weight, my life would work better than if I stopped controlling it. I didn't realize that the eating disorder—the diet—was actually controlling me. I spent a little over a decade in this struggle before God began to reveal the truth to me. Once my eyes were opened to the sham it all had been, I became increasingly intent on breaking free.

I wanted freedom, but I wasn't sure where to begin. It didn't take long to realize that I needed someone whose counseling method was based on biblical truths, so I asked the Lord to lead me to the right one. He did, and I just continued taking the next right step in front of me. This led me to attend a recovery group (in which I was the only eating disordered person, but at least I was plugging into community).

Soon into the healing process, I got pregnant with my first son, Christian. Gaining weight in pregnancy helped quell some of my fears about what would happen if I didn't maintain a particular weight. From there it was a continued march forward. There were slipups along the way, but over time I took more steps forward than backward. That is the journey of recovery. You fall down and get back up again, but there is grace all along the way. The important thing is to give yourself time to move forward and to receive God's grace in the midst of your dark places. If you had to clean yourself up first, it would no longer be grace! Scripture says,

"'My grace is sufficient for you, for my power is made perfect in weakness.' Therefore I will boast all the more gladly about my weaknesses, so that Christ's power may rest on me" (2 Corinthians 12:9, NIV).

What advice would I give to other girls who are struggling? First, turning to an eating disorder to lose weight isn't going to solve your body-image issues. In fact, it will create new ones. Next, admit you have a problem and know that you are not alone. Today in my work at FINDING*balance*, group programs are a core element because I know all too well the power of recognizing you are not alone and of reaching out in honesty and transparency for help along the way. Until we get honest with others in community, we are unlikely to see God's power in action.

Also, consider that the more time you spend focusing on your body and your looks, the less time you have to invest in authentic relationships with others and even God. Romans 8:7 says that "focusing on the self is the opposite of focusing on God" (MSG). Because eating issues—like any secret sin—are inherently self-focused, there is a natural disruption in the flow of your relationship with God when you are engaged in them. This is a trap Satan wants you to fall into because he wants to steal your God-given identity and influence. Don't fall for his trap. You have been created with a purpose, and when you know your value, you can change your world. Choose to buck the culture's measures of value so that you can be a powerful change agent instead.

Today my faith in God's power has been strengthened by the journey He has taken me on. Revelation 12:11 tells us that we will overcome by the blood of the Lamb and the word of our testimony. As I look back on all that God has done—not only to

free me from this trap but also to then use me to free others—
I am increasingly overwhelmed with excitement and gratitude
for His power and goodness. This is what happens as we allow
God to rescue and heal us. It propels us into a new, life-giving
cycle, which over time replaces the old ones we thought we'd
never escape.

## CHAPTER 8

# Can I Get a Little Help Here?

In Jesus' three short years of visible ministry, He healed a lot of people. Tons of them. In fact, crowds of people would follow Him, swarm Him, get all up in His space, holding on to the hope that maybe, just maybe, they might be one of those healed. Men and women young and old cried out to Him, "Have mercy, Jesus!" They begged Him to heal them or someone they loved. Jesus had compassion on the crowds of sick and dying people. He saw their desperation, and their faith moved Him to act. We read story after story in the Gospels of people asking and Jesus responding.

But one story was different. One man didn't ask to be healed. In fact, Jesus asked *him* that question instead:

Inside [Jerusalem], near the Sheep Gate, was the
pool of Bethesda, with five covered porches. Crowds
of sick people—blind, lame, or paralyzed—lay on
the porches. One of the men lying there had been
sick for thirty-eight years. When Jesus saw him and
knew he had been ill for a long time, he asked him,
"Would you like to get well?" JOHN 5:2-6

At first glance, I'm tempted to call Jesus out for stating the
obvious. All those sick people lay on the porches around the
pool of Bethesda precisely *because* they wanted to get well. It's
not like they didn't have anything better to do; they were there
for a reason. See, there was a legend about that pool. Some
people believed that every so often an angel would come and
stir up the water. When he did, the first person to race into the
pool would be healed. Did this man want to be healed? Given
he was willing to lie on a thin mat camped out at Bethesda for
who knows how long, you'd think so. But one thing I know
about my Savior, He never spoke careless words. When Jesus
spoke, He had His reasons. So as I read this story, I have to
ask myself, *Why would Jesus ask if the man wanted to get well?*

I have a hunch. Now, I admit this is speculation. The
Bible doesn't tell us exactly why He asked. But while walking alongside many girls who have struggled to let go of the
sin in their lives, I've seen something that might shed light
into Jesus' question. I think Jesus asked the man whether
he wanted to get well because deep down the man wasn't
sure. He had been sick for—count 'em—*thirty-eight years!*

Here's the deal. When we've been "sick" for a long time, sometimes healing is scarier than sickness. The "mat" we're lying on is familiar. It doesn't require effort. People feel bad for us and show us pity when we're lying on our sickbed. And then there's the fear of failure: If we actually try to stand up, as Jesus later commanded the man, we're afraid it might not work. We fear being embarrassed or disappointed if we step out in faith but then fall ill again. And as long as we're lying on our mats, we can stay attached to our pet lies. Such thoughts as *I'm not good enough*, *I'm never going to change*, and *I'm too far gone to turn around* can feel like warm, fuzzy blankets—familiar and soothing. (Of course, those lies eventually strangle the life right out of us, more like a python than a blanket.) But if we were healed, we would have to make the effort to replace those well-rehearsed lies with God's bold, uncompromising truth.

I hear the hesitation in the man's voice as he answered Jesus:

> "I can't, sir," the sick man said, "for I have no one
> to put me into the pool when the water bubbles up.
> Someone else always gets there ahead of me."
> JOHN 5:7

Instead of answering Jesus' question (whether he *wanted* to be healed), the man told Jesus why he *couldn't* be healed.

So Jesus asked the question again, a different way, this time testing whether the man truly wanted healing by offering it to him:

> Jesus told him, "Stand up, pick up your mat, and walk!"
>
> JOHN 5:8

Now the ball was in this sick man's court. If he truly wanted healing, he would have to act. Jesus required him to play an active role in his own healing—even though in this case it was on the Sabbath, which was against the Jewish rules. If the man wanted to be well, he would have to trust Jesus, physically stand up, roll up his sleeping mat, and take a literal step of faith.

I'm happy to report that this story has a very happy ending. The man exercised his faith. He rolled up that straw mat and began walking for the first time in decades. Can you picture it? Imagine how ecstatic he must have been. Man, I get goose bumps thinking about it! But not only did Jesus physically heal the man, He also addressed the state of his heart. Later that day, Jesus found the man again and said, "Now you are well; so stop sinning" (verse 14). Jesus knew that the man would only truly be healed when his heart matched his new, healthy body. The same is true for us.

We've traveled a good ways now down the road toward healing. I've tried my best to present God's truth about sin, shame, freedom, victory, and the importance of staying connected to God. You've heard the truth. So let me ask you this:

*Do you want to get well?*

A simple question; maybe a difficult answer. Are you truly willing to face the fear of getting off your familiar mat, the fear of failure, the fear of the unknown? Are you willing to do whatever it takes to live in the light of freedom—of wellness? And here's one more question: Are you willing to get outside help if that's what it takes?

## Calling for Reinforcements

I've included this chapter to share some practical places you can go if you need more help on this journey toward freedom. But before I introduce them, I ask you to consider this: If you've been "sick" for a long time (as many of those with secret sins have been), Jesus may ask you to take a step of faith. He may test your resolve. He may ask you to prove that you're willing to do your part, because it's way easier to pray, "God, please heal me," than to pray, "God, show me the steps you want me to take, no matter how hard they may be." Right? And as much as we would all love to have an instantaneous, miraculous, and complete healing from the effects of our sin, more often Jesus takes us the long way home. The business He wants to do in our hearts often takes time. And it often takes help.

We've already talked a bit about allowing others in— about involving them in your journey. Remember, the solo sin-slayer is a myth. You need to confess your sins to a person you trust and enlist the help of someone who can keep you accountable. However, if you've taken those steps and you're still struggling, aren't seeing progress, feel depressed, or are on the verge of giving up, it might be time to take another step of faith by calling for reinforcements. See, I'm older and wiser now, and if I knew then (when I was trapped in cycles of sin) what I know now, there's no way I would have hidden my junk for so many years. I would have hunted down some help pronto. And I would have used one criterion to figure out which help to get.

## Spotting a Counterfeit

As you start searching for help, you'll likely find well-meaning people giving really bad advice. You'll find programs, doctors, and resources that make promises they can't keep. You might even run across bizarre rituals or wacky diets. So when you know you need help, the first order of business is to find something that will actually help (not groom you to be a witch doctor or something).

The sheer volume of resources out there can be overwhelming. In that sea of "fixes," how will you know where to begin? How will you know which sources to trust?

When governments train their federal agents to spot counterfeit money, they don't start out by explaining all the different ways crooks print phony bills. Instead, agents study the real thing. They get to know the feel of the paper, the identifying holograms and unique lines that make that bill genuine. They become experts of the real thing so that anything fake grabs their attention.[1] In the spiritual world, we call that discernment. When we know God's truth like the back of our hand, any method, program, or promise that isn't truth will just feel off.

First Thessalonians 5:21-22 says, "Test everything that is

said. Hold on to what is good. Stay away from every kind of evil." You have the responsibility to test everything you come across against God's standard of truth. So if your roommate comes to you and says you'd feel better in a jiffy if you'd just give TM (Transcendental Meditation) a try, you'll spot the danger right away. As soon as she instructs you to recite a mantra (a Hindu holy word) over and over or points you to a "higher level of consciousness" to fix your issues, the alarm bells will go off. You'll remember that God's Word says to fill your mind with truth, not empty it of reason (see Romans 12:1-2), and that true freedom is found in God's truth, not a mental state (see John 8:32).

But I recognize that at this point in your journey it might be hard to spot a counterfeit. You may not know your Bible cover to cover yet, which means you'll have to lean on godly men and women (who've been doing this Christianity thing a wee bit longer) to steer you in the right direction. That's where I come in. And believe me, I take that responsibility very seriously!

## Where You'd Find Me

Because you have unique experiences and tendencies and a personality all your own, I can't offer a one-size-fits-all plan for getting the help you need, if you need it. I'm most certainly not here to force a particular method, treatment, or program on you. For one, I don't know all that's out there. Two, I'm still figuring out a lot of stuff for myself! So I entrust the responsibility of finding the best help for you to you. However, I *can* tell you where you'd find me if I got caught up in a cycle of sin and shame again. If I were struggling to kick a sin habit or losing a battle against intense emotions and not seeing any progress, I'd start by finding accountability.

## Accountability

*Accountability? Haven't we already covered that, Jessie?* Yeah, I know. But if I continued to flounder while having one person hold me accountable, I would carefully select additional support. Breaking a sin habit goes back to reward, remember? So if the reward of not disappointing one person weren't enough to forego sinful pleasure, maybe the reward of not having to fess up to three might do the trick!

All kidding aside, I believe there is strength in numbers. When you have multiple people praying for your healing, God takes notice. He also notices one person's prayers, but Jesus did say, "If two of you agree here on earth concerning anything you ask, my Father in heaven will do it for you" (Matthew 18:19). So the more people praying for your freedom, the better.

I also think of a story that you'll know well if you went to Sunday school as a kid. Remember the four friends who crashed a party by digging a huge hole in some guy's roof so they could lower their sick friend to Jesus? Have you ever chewed on Jesus' reaction to their unconventional antics? "Seeing *their* faith, Jesus said to the paralyzed man, 'My child, your sins are forgiven'" (Mark 2:5, emphasis added). Jesus didn't heal the paralyzed man because *he* had tremendous faith to be healed; Jesus took pity on him because of his *friends'* faith. Those are the kinds of friends I want to have: people who will carry me to Jesus if I don't have the strength or smarts to cry out to Him on my own. *That's* why I'd seek out more accountability.

## Resources

Being held accountable by multiple people and still not finding complete freedom would cause me to start finding other helpful resources. Remember when we said that sometimes media can be good and helpful? This is one of those times. We have access to tons of books, videos, website articles, social media threads, and music that have the ability to convict us, teach us, and create an atmosphere of faith in our lives. If I were at a dead end, I would start saturating myself in those resources. I know it's hard to resist our favorite TV shows, magazines, and music (because they're fun and entertaining) and replace them with meatier stuff, but desperate times call for desperate measures. If you want to be well, are you willing to take a step of faith by giving up your "right" to entertainment so you'll have more time to focus on God?

This is where that discernment piece really comes into play. There are a lot of resources from well-meaning people who can do a lot of damage to our minds and hearts, so choose your sources carefully. Find Bible teachers, authors, and musicians who are committed to God's Word and to helping others live in His light, not spouting man-made, well-wishing mumbo jumbo.

## Dietician

You might be surprised by the connection between food and your general well-being. (I was.) Sometimes the simple things in life can make a really big difference. The foods (or lack thereof) we put into our bodies have the ability to alter our moods, energy levels, sleep patterns, and overall ability to cope with the ups and downs of life. (That's important to understand because, as you'll remember, many of our secret sins are ways to cope.) So if I were calling for reinforcements in my fight against sin (or depression), I'd enlist the help of a dietician. If I couldn't afford to pay a dietician, I'd go back to "resources" and start reading up on food allergies, optimum nutrition, and natural, plant-based diets. (Again, this might not be for everyone, but it's where *I* would go if I needed extra support.)

## Pastor/Biblical Counselor or Group Program

If I *still* didn't experience complete freedom, I'd join a group program or look for and ask to meet regularly with a pastor or biblical counselor. Any of these options can help us tackle emotional and behavioral issues at their source: our hearts. So much of what we face, particularly when it comes to secret sins, can be traced to lies we believe about God, about ourselves, and about our world. It can be helpful to have someone trained to use God's Word (Truth with a capital *T*) to help us cut through and peel back layers of lies and beliefs that have kept us tied up.

If you decide to go this route, do some homework before you commit to a group or individual. Make sure the program or counselor has both credentials and faith. You want an individual or group leader you feel comfortable with, who isn't afraid to tell you hard truths when necessary, and who has an active, vibrant relationship with Jesus.

## Residential Counseling Center

If I had met regularly with a pastor or biblical counselor and still didn't see lasting change and freedom in my life, I'd start looking for a residential counseling center. Sometimes it takes getting out of our familiar surroundings to get a fresh perspective on our lives and on our struggles. I experienced this every year on a small scale when I went to a Christian summer camp as a teenager. Up in the mountains, free from the distractions of home, being fed from God's Word morning and night—after just a week, the transformation in my heart was dramatic! A live-in center is kind of like that. You get to experience the Lord in new ways as you step out from the familiar, all the while being surrounded by staff there for the sole purpose of helping you find freedom.

There's no shame in running hard after freedom, even if you have to go to greater lengths than others to find it. Will some people misunderstand or judge you if you go to counseling or move to a residential center? Maybe. But in the big picture, does that really matter? If you're not sure whether you're willing to go "that far," let me ask you again: Do you want to get well? If you do, be willing to step out in faith. Be willing to follow where God leads. Let's not sacrifice the freedom God wants for us because we're afraid someone might judge. Deal?

Not sure where to begin? Find examples of resources, biblical counseling services, group programs, and residential counseling centers at www.LifeLoveandGod.com/unashamed.

Proverbs 18:14 says, "The human spirit can endure a sick body, but who can bear a crushed spirit?" I agree with Solomon: Even a puke-your-guts-out flu has nothing on a "crushed spirit." Whether your emotional pain comes from circumstances, shame over sin, perfectionism, or any combination of sources, the pain can feel like sickness. If you want to get well—if you're sick of your sin, and sick of lying on your mat hoping for a miracle, and sick of the pain, and sick of feeling as though nothing is ever going to change, and just sick, sick, sick of it all—then are you willing to do whatever it takes to be made well?

Are you ready to stand wobbly kneed, roll up your sickbed, and take one purposeful step of faith?

There are people who care about you—people who want to see you made well. Reach out to them. Let them help. Tell them your needs and accept their aid. There ain't no shame in calling for reinforcements in our war against sin and against Satan!

Other people can help. But even more so, your Savior can—your Savior, who wants your freedom so badly that He's willing to initiate the conversation and ask you, "Do you want to be made well?"

Remember Psalm 34? Verse 18 is one of my all-time favorites: "The LORD is close to the brokenhearted; he rescues those whose spirits are crushed." Will you let Him be close? Will you let Him rescue you? Are you ready to follow Jesus out of sickness and into freedom, even if that means reaching out for help?

> *Dear Lord, I want to be made well, but I'm not sure where to start. I know that even though You are enough, You sometimes work through other believers to speak truth into my life. Show me where to go and whom to trust. I'm serious about getting my life right with You, even if that means I have to venture outside my comfort zone. Your freedom and joy would be worth it, so I'm willing to take that step of faith. Be close to me in the journey; rescue me, God. Amen.*

## Discussion Questions

1. *What obstacles—physical, mental, or spiritual—keep you from stepping out in faith?*

2. If Jesus was here right now and asked you, "Do you want to be free from your sin?" how would you answer Him?

3. When you think of being completely free from your secret sin, does any part of you fear losing the familiarity of it? Are you afraid of failing? Are any other fears keeping you from "picking up your mat"?

4. How could you use the federal agents' model of detecting counterfeit money to help you spot counterfeit truth? How would that be helpful as you look for resources to help you in your journey to freedom?

5. Why do secret sins and depression often go hand in hand?

6. After reading this chapter, would you be willing to try any of the suggestions for getting outside help? Do you have any suggestions to add?

## CHAPTER 9

# A ~~Little~~ Big Thing Called Hope

Hope changes everything.

But not the kind of hope we're used to.

Our English word *hope* gets slapped on a huge range of wants, from soul-deep longing to petty wishful thinking. We hope our grandma gets well, and we hope we don't trip on the stairs to trig class. We hope to get married or that our team wins the big game or for a white Christmas. We hope it doesn't rain so our hair won't frizz out. And we hope children won't starve in Africa in almost the same breath we hope 7-Eleven isn't out of Slurpees. That kind of hope—the one-size-fits-all variety we're used to—can be shallow. It's limited to something we *do*.

But the kind of hope the Bible talks about (particularly in the New Testament) is different. It's not something we do; it's something we have. Not to get all technical on you, but it's important we get a handle on this (as you'll see). The Greek word for hope, *elpo*, is "a favorable and confident expectation, a forward look with assurance."[1] In other words, this kind of hope isn't wishful thinking; it's something we can get excited about now because we *know* it's going to happen later. It's a sure bet. And that kind of hope is powerful! Hebrews 6:19 says, "This hope is a strong and trustworthy anchor for our souls." An *anchor* for our souls.

Have you ever been sailing? I played around on a catamaran one summer, and though my nautical knowledge is pretty slim, I do understand the wind's power against a sail. (Said wind may have tipped my tiny vessel plumb over, dumping an embarrassed me right into the water—fully clothed.) A sailboat is at the mercy of the wind, waves, and currents of the ocean. If a storm blows in, even a trained sailor can be helpless against it. God bless the person who invented anchors! An anchor does for a sailor what he can't do for himself: Hold steady. Stay put. Ride out the storm. An anchor is the only way a boat can hold still on the constantly moving and changing surface of the water.

An anchored *soul*—now that would be pretty revolutionary, don't you think?

Can you imagine being able to hold steady when your family falls apart or you have feelings for someone you shouldn't? To stay put when your emotions threaten to sink your ship when there's a shooting at school or you fail at something really important? To ride out the storm when your life crumbles around you and you're not sure how you're going to make it through? This would be a serious hope!

Take another look at Hebrews 6:19. Notice it doesn't say that hope in general will anchor our souls; it says "*this* hope." So what hope is he talking about? What type of hope could possibly have that kind of power? According to the verses just before and after, this is our hope: God has given us a divine pinky promise that our future is safe with Him. And unlike your big brother or best friend, God never goes back on His promises. If you belong to Him, then you know the end of your life's story. You make it through okay! (Yes, that may be the biggest understatement of the entire book.) There's something powerful about knowing that no matter how bad life gets here on this sin-ravaged earth, in the end it all works out for God's glory and our good.

But there's more to this hope than just knowing "God wins" in the end.

The rest of Hebrews 6:19 explains that this soul-anchoring hope does something else: It "leads us through the curtain into God's inner sanctuary." Brief history lesson: In the Jewish Temple, a huge, thick curtain separated the holy place from the really-super-duper holy place—the place where God Himself hung out. God was serious about His space. That inner sanctuary was dubbed the Holy of Holies. Only the high priest could enter, and he could enter only once a year (on the Day of Atonement). All that to say, no one went into the inner sanctuary unless invited, or they'd die—literally. Now check this out: The writer of Hebrews is telling us that this hope gives us a VIP pass into God's private room.

Hope gives us access to God's very presence.

I realize that might sound mystical or churchy, so let me break it down by giving you three practical ways that hope gives us access to, or draws us closer to, God.

## The Hope of Beauty

My daughters love mermaids. When their grandparents gave them a lovely little mermaid figurine, they treasured that princess of the sea like she was the most beautiful thing they owned because, well, she *was*. But one day that beautiful, blue-tailed mermaid tumbled from the kitchen island onto the wood floor below with a mighty crash. The utter despair on their faces broke my heart, so I promised I'd try to fix her. Key word: *try*.

That glue job was way out of my league. I did my best. Really, I did. Armed with a tube of Elmer's, I tried to reconstruct that sweet little mermaid. But—poor thing—she was never the same. Her crooked tail, chipped crown, and fingerless hand gave away the fact that she was broken. Bad. And even though she was still precious to my daughters, my do-it-yourself repair job failed to restore her to her former beauty.

Lucky for us, God knows how to mend broken treasures way better than you or I do. In fact, He is an expert at *kintsugi*. Kintsugi is the Japanese art of fixing broken ceramics using a resin that looks like solid gold.[2] A kintsugi craftsman takes a broken piece of pottery and carefully joins the pieces together. But the seams aren't lumpy and jagged like my attempt to mend Miss Mermaid. These joints are smooth and precise and glisten like golden lightning bolts across an otherwise-bland pot or jug. After the kintsugi is finished, you don't just have a fixed bowl; you've got a work of art.

When God mends the broken pieces of your life, you are more beautiful for having been broken. He doesn't just make you beautiful *despite* your biggest mess-ups; He makes you beautiful *because* of them.

If sin has dropped you off a kitchen island, shattered you into pieces, and left you for the trash bin, don't believe the lie that you will never be whole or beautiful again. Granted, if you try to fix yourself, you'll probably end up with gloppy glue streaks and crooked features like my girls' mermaid. But if you hand the pieces of your life to the Master Mender, His kintsugi prowess won't just make you good as new; it will make you even better. He will make you a work of art by bringing greater strength to the very places of your heart that were once shattered:

> We can rejoice, too, when we run into problems and trials, for we know that they help us develop endurance. And endurance develops strength of character, and character strengthens our confident hope of salvation. And this hope will not lead to disappointment. ROMANS 5:3-5

Those "golden seams"—the places God has mended—are strong with character. And that stronger character expands our hope.

Like my girls as they stood over the broken pieces of their mermaid in tears, you might be staring at the fragments of your heart with utter despair. Or maybe you've already tried the do-it-yourself approach. Maybe you've been using sin as imitation glue—trying to hold it all together with a relationship, drug, or blade—and you're disappointed with the patchy results.

If that's you, then let hope usher you into God's presence. Let the assurance of God's promises draw you closer to Him. He promises to mend you and make you more beautiful than ever if you'll look to Him. Remember Psalm 34:5? It tells us, "Those who look to him for help will be radiant with joy; no shadow of shame will darken their faces." Those who look to Him will be radiant. Beautiful. Whole. Healed. Full of joy. *Unashamed*. Amen?

## The Hope of Helping

You were broken. You have hope because God makes beauty out of your brokenness. Now you have the hope of helping others.

Have you ever been really sad or hurt about something and then someone came along who just "got it" because they had been through something similar? I have. For instance, when my mom died, I appreciated every card, sympathetic word, and kind gesture *anyone* offered. But it was like I had this instant connection with women who had "been there"—anyone who had lost someone close to them and made it through the intense pain alive. They understood me. They had blown through their own boxes of tissues, all raccoon-eyed and blubbery. They had faced the future without someone they cared deeply for. They knew how I felt, and they had battle-tested advice for how to cling to God through that dark valley.

It's such a picture of how God's people (the church) should operate. Second Corinthians 1:4 says, "[God] comforts us in all our troubles *so that* we can comfort others. When they are troubled, we will be able to give them the same comfort God has given us" (emphasis added). The people who "got it" comforted me as no one else could because God had first done it for them. They knew the ropes, and now it was their turn to explain the intimidating course to me. And now that I've made it through, I have the responsibility (and joy) to be there for others in their deep pain. People who suffer the most get to give the most.

The same is true of your journey to freedom from your secret sin. After you break free from the dark chains of shame, regret, addiction, and hopelessness, you'll have the responsibility (and joy) of coming alongside other girls who are stuck in spiritual prison. You'll get to listen to, share with, and cry right alongside them. You'll know the ropes, and it will be your turn to guide others through the scary obstacles you overcame.

Some of the most rewarding experiences of my life have been giving others "the same comfort God has given [me]." And some of my happiest moments have been watching those girls walk in freedom and proclaim God's goodness and grace to others still. It's exhilarating to know you have played even a small part in someone else's freedom. And that's what you have to look forward to! God is comforting you in your pain so that you can offer that same comfort to others.

## The Hope of Heaven

The hope of heaven is perhaps the greatest of all. But before I tell you why, I need you to do something for me. I need you to gather any and all Precious Moments–esque, fluffy-cloud, cherub-filled ideas about heaven floating in your brain and chuck them out the window. Heaven—the *real* heaven—is nothing like the renditions we see in the movies or in Hallmark stores. It's not filled with mild-mannered, halo-wearing, pansy angels with wings. And heaven certainly isn't some boring country club where we sit around strumming harps ever after. It's way better than that.

If you're not familiar with what the real heaven is going to be like—aka the New Jerusalem—I recommend you read Revelation 21–22. Here's just a snippet to whet your appetite:

> I saw a new heaven and a new earth, for the old
> heaven and the old earth had disappeared. And the
> sea was also gone. And I saw the holy city, the new
> Jerusalem, coming down from God out of heaven
> like a bride beautifully dressed for her husband.

I heard a loud shout from the throne, saying,
"Look, God's home is now among his people! He
will live with them, and they will be his people. God
himself will be with them. He will wipe every tear from
their eyes, and there will be no more death or sorrow
or crying or pain. All these things are gone forever."
And the one sitting on the throne said, "Look,
I am making everything new!" . . . And he also said
. . . "To all who are thirsty I will give freely from the
springs of the water of life. All who are victorious
will inherit all these blessings, and I will be their
God, and they will be my children."

REVELATION 21:1-7

I'm really stoked about heaven for a lot of reasons, but there
are a few specific things about our eternal home that especially
excite me in light of all we've talked about in this book.

## #1: No more stupid sin!

In heaven, we'll be completely holy. That means there won't
be any part of us that's not pleasing to God. No more battle
between what we want to do (obey God) and what our flesh
wants to do (swim in sin). This is exceptional news because
you know what? Sometimes I'm just exhausted from the battle.
I get weary of struggling with the same old ugly sin—of taking two steps forward and one step back. I hate my sin! And
I'm really looking forward to being rid of it F-O-R-E-V-E-R.
How about you?

### #2: We'll share space with God Himself.

As we saw in the opening verses of Revelation 21, God is literally going to live with us in our new digs. A little later (verse 23), we learn that between God the Father and Jesus Christ, we won't need the sun, moon, flashlights, candles, or lightbulbs; His presence will be all the light we need. We're going to be so close to God that He'll light up our world! Can you imagine what it will be like to have the God of the universe living with us? Can you even comprehend an existence with "no more death or sorrow or crying or pain" (21:4)? A piece of my mind just blew a fuse. It's crazy, right?

As awesome as it will be to never again have to worry about messing up my mascara with the "ugly cry" (you *know* what I'm talking about), the thing I'm looking forward to most about heaven is just being with God. I've spent my whole life trying to know Him—trying to understand Him, trying to get close to Him, trying to please Him. All those attempts will be over. Done. Complete. When I finally get to see Him face-to-face, all my divine longings will be filled. I'll finally have *all* of Jesus I desire. That's the most exciting thing I can imagine.

### #3: We'll finally feel *true* rest.

I know I'm not the only one who sometimes feels as though life is just one event after another, one desire after another, one goal after another. It's like a merry-go-round of striving. Sometimes our entire existence feels like one epic struggle—

a race for meaning, money, success, and love. If you're caught in a cycle of sin, then I can pretty much guarantee you're not at rest! Something is always eating at you, making you anxious, even in life's happiest moments. But all that struggling will end in heaven: "God will provide rest for you . . . when the Lord Jesus appears from heaven" (2 Thessalonians 1:7).

We'll be *forever* at rest. That's even better than a late-spring nap on a sunny towel at the beach (which is as close to "rest" as I can imagine on this side of eternity). Heaven's kind of soul rest won't ever fade, and you'll never wake up from it. That sounds mighty appealing right about now.

We have hope because in God's upside-down kingdom, we grow to be beautiful *precisely because* we've been broken. We have hope because God can use even our biggest mistakes to help others. And we have hope because this life isn't all there is. In heaven we won't struggle with sin *anymore*. Woo-hoo!

Let hope—the hope of beauty, helping, and heaven—anchor your soul. Let it hold you steady when the storms hit. They *will* hit, and some of them will hit hard. But remember that God's kind of hope is a sure bet. He has promised to see you through this (see Philippians 1:6), and He never goes back on His word. As long as you look to Him, your ship—your life—won't sink.

This has been quite a journey, hasn't it? I have to tell you, this has been the hardest book I've ever written. That's not just because I (still) wrestle with airing my sin for all the world to read but also because I've hit roadblock after roadblock along the way. Let's just say Satan has not wanted it finished. I truly believe he fears the damage it's going to do to the strongholds he has on God's daughters. But I also believe, in faith, that God is going to use this book to bring freedom to silent sufferers around the world. And that makes it all worth it. *You are worth it.*

Don't give up the fight. No matter how deep the shame, no matter how hard the struggle, no matter how many times you fall flat on your face along the way, don't quit. Jesus has overcome the world (see John 16:33), and freedom is yours for the taking. Your jail cell is wide open. Fight your way out of sin and into the Light, where God's blessings flow wide and deep.

Live like the victor you are!

*God, thank You for the hope You've given me. I can't imagine trying to crawl out of this pit on my own, but I know that through You, I can do anything. Take the broken pieces of my life and craft them into something beautiful. And when that mending hurts and I feel like giving up, remind me of Your promises. Let everything I know about You and Your love for me hold me steady when storms hit. I love You, Father. Amen.*

# Discussion Questions

1. *How is the common English word* hope *different from biblical hope?*

2. *What storm are you facing in your life? How could hope anchor your soul through it?*

3. *How can hope usher you into God's presence, drawing you closer to Him?*

4. *How does* kintsugi *illustrate the hope of beauty we have in God?*

5. *How might God use the dark valleys you've been through to encourage and help others?*

6. What are you most looking forward to in heaven? Why?

7. Pull out your journal one last time. Write a letter or prayer to God thanking Him for the hope He has given you and asking for strength to continue walking with Him until you find complete freedom from your secret sins and beyond.

# Notes

## CHAPTER 1: THE SILENT SUFFERERS

1. If you have been abused in any way, please know that the abuse was not your fault. You are not responsible for that person's sin against you. However, each of us does have a choice of how we respond to abuse. We're going to talk more about our response in chapter 4.
2. We're going to talk about why it's wrong in chapter 2.
3. Malia Wollen, "San Francisco Officials Approve a Ban on Public Nudity," *The New York Times*, November 20, 2012, http://www.nytimes.com/2012/11/21/us/san-francisco-officials -vote-to-ban-public-nudity.html?_r=0.
4. *Merriam-Webster's*, 11th ed., s.v. "shame."
5. At least we *should* feel it down deep! But if we continue in a particular sin long enough, we can harden our conscience toward it. If that happens, it's possible to do wrong and not feel badly about it at all.
6. Name has been changed. Story used with permission.
7. James Strong, *The New Strong's Expanded Exhaustive Concordance of the Bible* (Nashville: Thomas Nelson, 2001), s.v. "*nâbat*," Hebrew #5027.

## CHAPTER 2: WHAT'S YOUR SECRET?

1. Jarryd Willis, "Understanding Cutting and Bullycide," *The Huffington Post*, July 19, 2013, http://www.huffingtonpost.com/jarryd-willis /self-injury_b_3536518.html.
2. Substance abuse. Dictionary.com. *The American Heritage® Stedman's Medical Dictionary*. Houghton Mifflin Company. http://dictionary .reference.com/browse/substance abuse (accessed August 25, 2013).

3. In biblical times, there were different types of wine. Some had much higher alcohol content than others, such as "red" or "mixed" wine (see Proverbs 23:29-35). Others were milder and people drank them for the probiotic benefits rather than a buzz (see 1 Timothy 5:23). Today you might compare the difference to a beer and a kombucha.

4. Although this is pretty common knowledge, one source is Anne M. Morris and Debra K. Katzman, "The Impact of the Media on Eating Disorders in Children and Adolescents," *Paediatrics & Child Health*, Pulsus Group, Inc., May–June (2003), 8(5): 287–289, accessed August 18, 2013, http://www.ncbi.nlm.nih.gov/pmc/articles /PMC2792687/#.

5. Some LGBT advocates argue that this verse describes what is normal, not necessarily what is normative. In other words, they would say that just because God started out with one man and one woman doesn't mean He won't *allow* men to choose men or women to choose women. But when Genesis 2 is combined with other passages (such as Leviticus 18, Romans 1:18-32, and 1 Corinthians 6:12-19), God's plan for guy + girl becomes clear.

6. *HCSB Study Bible* (Nashville: Holman Bible Publishers, 2010), 1883.

### CHAPTER 3: THE DISCONNECT

1. Lady Gaga, feat. R. Kelly, "Do What U Want," *Artpop* (Interscope Records, November 2013).

2. Based on Galatians 5:19-21.

3. Based on Galatians 5:22-23.

### CHAPTER 4: CALLING SIN *SIN* AND LEARNING TO FORGIVE

1. See 1 John 2:27; Romans 8:2; Ephesians 4:23.

2. James Strong, *The New Strong's Expanded Exhaustive Concordance of the Bible* (Nashville: Thomas Nelson, 2001), s.v. "*paideia*," Greek #3809.

3. Hebrews 12:8 says that God disciplines all of His children, which would include Jesus, who never did *anything* wrong. In Hebrews 5:8, we read that Jesus "learned obedience through what He suffered" (HCSB). Because He never sinned, His suffering couldn't have been punishment.

### CHAPTER 5: LET FREEDOM RING

1. Except where noted, the information used for this story is from "Juneteenth: Our Other Independence Day," by Kenneth C. Davis, Smithsonian.com, June 15, 2011, http://www.smithsonianmag.com /history-archaeology/Juneteenth-Our-Other-Independence-Day.html.

2. "Juneteenth," Texas State Library and Archives Commission, accessed October 6, 2013, https://www.tsl.state.tx.us/ref/abouttx/juneteenth.html.

## CHAPTER 6: KICKING THE HABIT

1. John Tierney, "The Rational Choices of Crack Addicts," *New York Times*, September 16, 2013, http://www.nytimes.com/2013/09/17/science/the-rational-choices-of-crack-addicts.html?pagewanted=all&_r=1&.

2. See Judges 11:29; 14–15; Acts 8:39; Romans 1:4.

## CHAPTER 7: MERCY FOR A FALL

1. Ephesians 2:8-9, Romans 5:16, and Romans 6:23 all clearly explain that salvation is a free gift from God. There is nothing we can do to earn it. But Satan knows that trying to earn our salvation will turn us into religious strivers, crippling our faith, which is why he'd love for us to believe that lie.

2. Constance Rhodes, *Life Inside the "Thin" Cage: A Personal Look into the Hidden World of the Chronic Dieter* (Colorado Springs, CO: WaterBrook, 2003).

## CHAPTER 8: CAN I GET A LITTLE HELP HERE?

1. Tim Challies, "Counterfeit Detection (Part 1)," June 27, 2006, http://www.challies.com/articles/counterfeit-detection-part-1.

## CHAPTER 9: A L̶I̶T̶T̶L̶E̶ BIG THING CALLED HOPE

1. James Strong, *The New Strong's Expanded Exhaustive Concordance of the Bible* (Nashville: Thomas Nelson, 2001), s.v. "*elpo*," Greek #1680.

2. Blake Gopnik, "'Golden Seams: The Japanese Art of Mending Ceramics' at Freer," *Washington Post*, March 3, 2009, http://www.washingtonpost.com/wp-dyn/content/article/2009/03/02/AR2009030202723.html.

# YOU'VE GOT QUESTIONS,
## JESSIE HAS ANSWERS

AVAILABLE AT NAVPRESS.COM
OR WHEREVER CHRISTIAN BOOKS ARE SOLD.

CP0875

# YOU'VE GOT QUESTIONS.
# JESSIE HAS ANSWERS.

## Connect with Jessie at
# LifeLoveandGod.com

**WHERE GIRLS ASK AND GET ANSWERS TO QUESTIONS**
**ABOUT BOYS, FAMILY, FRIENDS, AND GOD.**

 facebook.com/lifeloveNGod

pinterest.com/lifeloveandGod

twitter.com/lifeloveandGod

CP0769